C-2594   CAREER EXAMINATION SERIES

This is your
PASSBOOK for...

Senior Office Assistant

Test Preparation Study Guide
Questions & Answers

COPYRIGHT NOTICE

This book is SOLELY intended for, is sold ONLY to, and its use is RESTRICTED to individual, bona fide applicants or candidates who qualify by virtue of having seriously filed applications for appropriate license, certificate, professional and/or promotional advancement, higher school matriculation, scholarship, or other legitimate requirements of education and/or governmental authorities.

This book is NOT intended for use, class instruction, tutoring, training, duplication, copying, reprinting, excerption, or adaptation, etc., by:

1) Other publishers
2) Proprietors and/or Instructors of "Coaching" and/or Preparatory Courses
3) Personnel and/or Training Divisions of commercial, industrial, and governmental organizations
4) Schools, colleges, or universities and/or their departments and staffs, including teachers and other personnel
5) Testing Agencies or Bureaus
6) Study groups which seek by the purchase of a single volume to copy and/or duplicate and/or adapt this material for use by the group as a whole without having purchased individual volumes for each of the members of the group
7) Et al.

Such persons would be in violation of appropriate Federal and State statutes.

PROVISION OF LICENSING AGREEMENTS – Recognized educational, commercial, industrial, and governmental institutions and organizations, and others legitimately engaged in educational pursuits, including training, testing, and measurement activities, may address request for a licensing agreement to the copyright owners, who will determine whether, and under what conditions, including fees and charges, the materials in this book may be used them. In other words, a licensing facility exists for the legitimate use of the material in this book on other than an individual basis. However, it is asseverated and affirmed here that the material in this book CANNOT be used without the receipt of the express permission of such a licensing agreement from the Publishers. Inquiries re licensing should be addressed to the company, attention rights and permissions department.

All rights reserved, including the right of reproduction in whole or in part, in any form or by any means, electronic or mechanical, including photocopying, recording, or by any information storage and retrieval system, without permission in writing from the Publisher.

Copyright © 2024 by
National Learning Corporation

212 Michael Drive, Syosset, NY 11791
(516) 921-8888 • www.passbooks.com
E-mail: info@passbooks.com

PUBLISHED IN THE UNITED STATES OF AMERICA

PASSBOOK® SERIES

THE *PASSBOOK® SERIES* has been created to prepare applicants and candidates for the ultimate academic battlefield – the examination room.

At some time in our lives, each and every one of us may be required to take an examination – for validation, matriculation, admission, qualification, registration, certification, or licensure.

Based on the assumption that every applicant or candidate has met the basic formal educational standards, has taken the required number of courses, and read the necessary texts, the *PASSBOOK® SERIES* furnishes the one special preparation which may assure passing with confidence, instead of failing with insecurity. Examination questions – together with answers – are furnished as the basic vehicle for study so that the mysteries of the examination and its compounding difficulties may be eliminated or diminished by a sure method.

This book is meant to help you pass your examination provided that you qualify and are serious in your objective.

The entire field is reviewed through the huge store of content information which is succinctly presented through a provocative and challenging approach – the question-and-answer method.

A climate of success is established by furnishing the correct answers at the end of each test.

You soon learn to recognize types of questions, forms of questions, and patterns of questioning. You may even begin to anticipate expected outcomes.

You perceive that many questions are repeated or adapted so that you can gain acute insights, which may enable you to score many sure points.

You learn how to confront new questions, or types of questions, and to attack them confidently and work out the correct answers.

You note objectives and emphases, and recognize pitfalls and dangers, so that you may make positive educational adjustments.

Moreover, you are kept fully informed in relation to new concepts, methods, practices, and directions in the field.

You discover that you are actually taking the examination all the time: you are preparing for the examination by "taking" an examination, not by reading extraneous and/or supererogatory textbooks.

In short, this PASSBOOK®, used directedly, should be an important factor in helping you to pass your test.

SENIOR OFFICE ASSISTANT

DUTIES
An employee in this class performs a variety of difficult and responsible clerical and typing functions. The principal emphasis of this position is upon the wide variety of clerical tasks performed, which require the application of independent judgment and clerical knowledge. The nature of the work is such that the incumbent may be required to operate a variety of office equipment. Supervision may be exercised over a small number of employees assisting in routine details. Work is performed under general supervision and is reviewed by a supervisor through observation of results, periodic audits of work performed and by advice and assistance on unusual problems. Does related work as required.

SCOPE OF THE EXAMINATION
The written test will cover knowledge, skills and abilities in such areas as:

1. Understanding and interpreting written material
2. Clerical operations, including proofreading; and
3. Office record keeping, including charts and numbers.

HOW TO TAKE A TEST

I. YOU MUST PASS AN EXAMINATION

A. WHAT EVERY CANDIDATE SHOULD KNOW
Examination applicants often ask us for help in preparing for the written test. What can I study in advance? What kinds of questions will be asked? How will the test be given? How will the papers be graded?

As an applicant for a civil service examination, you may be wondering about some of these things. Our purpose here is to suggest effective methods of advance study and to describe civil service examinations.

Your chances for success on this examination can be increased if you know how to prepare. Those "pre-examination jitters" can be reduced if you know what to expect. You can even experience an adventure in good citizenship if you know why civil service exams are given.

B. WHY ARE CIVIL SERVICE EXAMINATIONS GIVEN?
Civil service examinations are important to you in two ways. As a citizen, you want public jobs filled by employees who know how to do their work. As a job seeker, you want a fair chance to compete for that job on an equal footing with other candidates. The best-known means of accomplishing this two-fold goal is the competitive examination.

Exams are widely publicized throughout the nation. They may be administered for jobs in federal, state, city, municipal, town or village governments or agencies.

Any citizen may apply, with some limitations, such as the age or residence of applicants. Your experience and education may be reviewed to see whether you meet the requirements for the particular examination. When these requirements exist, they are reasonable and applied consistently to all applicants. Thus, a competitive examination may cause you some uneasiness now, but it is your privilege and safeguard.

C. HOW ARE CIVIL SERVICE EXAMS DEVELOPED?
Examinations are carefully written by trained technicians who are specialists in the field known as "psychological measurement," in consultation with recognized authorities in the field of work that the test will cover. These experts recommend the subject matter areas or skills to be tested; only those knowledges or skills important to your success on the job are included. The most reliable books and source materials available are used as references. Together, the experts and technicians judge the difficulty level of the questions.

Test technicians know how to phrase questions so that the problem is clearly stated. Their ethics do not permit "trick" or "catch" questions. Questions may have been tried out on sample groups, or subjected to statistical analysis, to determine their usefulness.

Written tests are often used in combination with performance tests, ratings of training and experience, and oral interviews. All of these measures combine to form the best-known means of finding the right person for the right job.

II. HOW TO PASS THE WRITTEN TEST

A. NATURE OF THE EXAMINATION

To prepare intelligently for civil service examinations, you should know how they differ from school examinations you have taken. In school you were assigned certain definite pages to read or subjects to cover. The examination questions were quite detailed and usually emphasized memory. Civil service exams, on the other hand, try to discover your present ability to perform the duties of a position, plus your potentiality to learn these duties. In other words, a civil service exam attempts to predict how successful you will be. Questions cover such a broad area that they cannot be as minute and detailed as school exam questions.

In the public service similar kinds of work, or positions, are grouped together in one "class." This process is known as *position-classification*. All the positions in a class are paid according to the salary range for that class. One class title covers all of these positions, and they are all tested by the same examination.

B. FOUR BASIC STEPS

1) Study the announcement

How, then, can you know what subjects to study? Our best answer is: "Learn as much as possible about the class of positions for which you've applied." The exam will test the knowledge, skills and abilities needed to do the work.

Your most valuable source of information about the position you want is the official exam announcement. This announcement lists the training and experience qualifications. Check these standards and apply only if you come reasonably close to meeting them.

The brief description of the position in the examination announcement offers some clues to the subjects which will be tested. Think about the job itself. Review the duties in your mind. Can you perform them, or are there some in which you are rusty? Fill in the blank spots in your preparation.

Many jurisdictions preview the written test in the exam announcement by including a section called "Knowledge and Abilities Required," "Scope of the Examination," or some similar heading. Here you will find out specifically what fields will be tested.

2) Review your own background

Once you learn in general what the position is all about, and what you need to know to do the work, ask yourself which subjects you already know fairly well and which need improvement. You may wonder whether to concentrate on improving your strong areas or on building some background in your fields of weakness. When the announcement has specified "some knowledge" or "considerable knowledge," or has used adjectives like "beginning principles of…" or "advanced … methods," you can get a clue as to the number and difficulty of questions to be asked in any given field. More questions, and hence broader coverage, would be included for those subjects which are more important in the work. Now weigh your strengths and weaknesses against the job requirements and prepare accordingly.

3) Determine the level of the position

Another way to tell how intensively you should prepare is to understand the level of the job for which you are applying. Is it the entering level? In other words, is this the position in which beginners in a field of work are hired? Or is it an intermediate or advanced level? Sometimes this is indicated by such words as "Junior" or "Senior" in the class title. Other jurisdictions use Roman numerals to designate the level – Clerk I, Clerk II, for example. The word "Supervisor" sometimes appears in the title. If the level is not indicated by the title, check the description of duties. Will you be working under very close supervision, or will you have responsibility for independent decisions in this work?

4) Choose appropriate study materials

Now that you know the subjects to be examined and the relative amount of each subject to be covered, you can choose suitable study materials. For beginning level jobs, or even advanced ones, if you have a pronounced weakness in some aspect of your training, read a modern, standard textbook in that field. Be sure it is up to date and has general coverage. Such books are normally available at your library, and the librarian will be glad to help you locate one. For entry-level positions, questions of appropriate difficulty are chosen – neither highly advanced questions, nor those too simple. Such questions require careful thought but not advanced training.

If the position for which you are applying is technical or advanced, you will read more advanced, specialized material. If you are already familiar with the basic principles of your field, elementary textbooks would waste your time. Concentrate on advanced textbooks and technical periodicals. Think through the concepts and review difficult problems in your field.

These are all general sources. You can get more ideas on your own initiative, following these leads. For example, training manuals and publications of the government agency which employs workers in your field can be useful, particularly for technical and professional positions. A letter or visit to the government department involved may result in more specific study suggestions, and certainly will provide you with a more definite idea of the exact nature of the position you are seeking.

III. KINDS OF TESTS

Tests are used for purposes other than measuring knowledge and ability to perform specified duties. For some positions, it is equally important to test ability to make adjustments to new situations or to profit from training. In others, basic mental abilities not dependent on information are essential. Questions which test these things may not appear as pertinent to the duties of the position as those which test for knowledge and information. Yet they are often highly important parts of a fair examination. For very general questions, it is almost impossible to help you direct your study efforts. What we can do is to point out some of the more common of these general abilities needed in public service positions and describe some typical questions.

1) General information

Broad, general information has been found useful for predicting job success in some kinds of work. This is tested in a variety of ways, from vocabulary lists to questions about current events. Basic background in some field of work, such as sociology or economics, may be sampled in a group of questions. Often these are principles which have become familiar to most persons through exposure rather than through formal training. It is difficult to advise you how to study for these questions; being alert to the world around you is our best suggestion.

2) Verbal ability

An example of an ability needed in many positions is verbal or language ability. Verbal ability is, in brief, the ability to use and understand words. Vocabulary and grammar tests are typical measures of this ability. Reading comprehension or paragraph interpretation questions are common in many kinds of civil service tests. You are given a paragraph of written material and asked to find its central meaning.

3) Numerical ability

Number skills can be tested by the familiar arithmetic problem, by checking paired lists of numbers to see which are alike and which are different, or by interpreting charts and graphs. In the latter test, a graph may be printed in the test booklet which you are asked to use as the basis for answering questions.

4) Observation

A popular test for law-enforcement positions is the observation test. A picture is shown to you for several minutes, then taken away. Questions about the picture test your ability to observe both details and larger elements.

5) Following directions

In many positions in the public service, the employee must be able to carry out written instructions dependably and accurately. You may be given a chart with several columns, each column listing a variety of information. The questions require you to carry out directions involving the information given in the chart.

6) Skills and aptitudes

Performance tests effectively measure some manual skills and aptitudes. When the skill is one in which you are trained, such as typing or shorthand, you can practice. These tests are often very much like those given in business school or high school courses. For many of the other skills and aptitudes, however, no short-time preparation can be made. Skills and abilities natural to you or that you have developed throughout your lifetime are being tested.

Many of the general questions just described provide all the data needed to answer the questions and ask you to use your reasoning ability to find the answers. Your best preparation for these tests, as well as for tests of facts and ideas, is to be at your physical and mental best. You, no doubt, have your own methods of getting into an exam-taking mood and keeping "in shape." The next section lists some ideas on this subject.

IV. KINDS OF QUESTIONS

Only rarely is the "essay" question, which you answer in narrative form, used in civil service tests. Civil service tests are usually of the short-answer type. Full instructions for answering these questions will be given to you at the examination. But in case this is your first experience with short-answer questions and separate answer sheets, here is what you need to know:

1) Multiple-choice Questions

Most popular of the short-answer questions is the "multiple choice" or "best answer" question. It can be used, for example, to test for factual knowledge, ability to solve problems or judgment in meeting situations found at work.

A multiple-choice question is normally one of three types—
- It can begin with an incomplete statement followed by several possible endings. You are to find the one ending which *best* completes the statement, although some of the others may not be entirely wrong.
- It can also be a complete statement in the form of a question which is answered by choosing one of the statements listed.

- It can be in the form of a problem – again you select the best answer.

Here is an example of a multiple-choice question with a discussion which should give you some clues as to the method for choosing the right answer:

When an employee has a complaint about his assignment, the action which will *best* help him overcome his difficulty is to
 A. discuss his difficulty with his coworkers
 B. take the problem to the head of the organization
 C. take the problem to the person who gave him the assignment
 D. say nothing to anyone about his complaint

In answering this question, you should study each of the choices to find which is best. Consider choice "A" – Certainly an employee may discuss his complaint with fellow employees, but no change or improvement can result, and the complaint remains unresolved. Choice "B" is a poor choice since the head of the organization probably does not know what assignment you have been given, and taking your problem to him is known as "going over the head" of the supervisor. The supervisor, or person who made the assignment, is the person who can clarify it or correct any injustice. Choice "C" is, therefore, correct. To say nothing, as in choice "D," is unwise. Supervisors have and interest in knowing the problems employees are facing, and the employee is seeking a solution to his problem.

2) True/False Questions

The "true/false" or "right/wrong" form of question is sometimes used. Here a complete statement is given. Your job is to decide whether the statement is right or wrong.

SAMPLE: A roaming cell-phone call to a nearby city costs less than a non-roaming call to a distant city.

This statement is wrong, or false, since roaming calls are more expensive.

This is not a complete list of all possible question forms, although most of the others are variations of these common types. You will always get complete directions for answering questions. Be sure you understand *how* to mark your answers – ask questions until you do.

V. RECORDING YOUR ANSWERS

Computer terminals are used more and more today for many different kinds of exams.

For an examination with very few applicants, you may be told to record your answers in the test booklet itself. Separate answer sheets are much more common. If this separate answer sheet is to be scored by machine – and this is often the case – it is highly important that you mark your answers correctly in order to get credit.

An electronic scoring machine is often used in civil service offices because of the speed with which papers can be scored. Machine-scored answer sheets must be marked with a pencil, which will be given to you. This pencil has a high graphite content which responds to the electronic scoring machine. As a matter of fact, stray dots may register as answers, so do not let your pencil rest on the answer sheet while you are pondering the correct answer. Also, if your pencil lead breaks or is otherwise defective, ask for another.

Since the answer sheet will be dropped in a slot in the scoring machine, be careful not to bend the corners or get the paper crumpled.

The answer sheet normally has five vertical columns of numbers, with 30 numbers to a column. These numbers correspond to the question numbers in your test booklet. After each number, going across the page are four or five pairs of dotted lines. These short dotted lines have small letters or numbers above them. The first two pairs may also have a "T" or "F" above the letters. This indicates that the first two pairs only are to be used if the questions are of the true-false type. If the questions are multiple choice, disregard the "T" and "F" and pay attention only to the small letters or numbers.

Answer your questions in the manner of the sample that follows:

32. The largest city in the United States is
    A. Washington, D.C.
    B. New York City
    C. Chicago
    D. Detroit
    E. San Francisco

1) Choose the answer you think is best. (New York City is the largest, so "B" is correct.)
2) Find the row of dotted lines numbered the same as the question you are answering. (Find row number 32)
3) Find the pair of dotted lines corresponding to the answer. (Find the pair of lines under the mark "B.")
4) Make a solid black mark between the dotted lines.

VI. BEFORE THE TEST

Common sense will help you find procedures to follow to get ready for an examination. Too many of us, however, overlook these sensible measures. Indeed, nervousness and fatigue have been found to be the most serious reasons why applicants fail to do their best on civil service tests. Here is a list of reminders:

- Begin your preparation early – Don't wait until the last minute to go scurrying around for books and materials or to find out what the position is all about.
- Prepare continuously – An hour a night for a week is better than an all-night cram session. This has been definitely established. What is more, a night a week for a month will return better dividends than crowding your study into a shorter period of time.
- Locate the place of the exam – You have been sent a notice telling you when and where to report for the examination. If the location is in a different town or otherwise unfamiliar to you, it would be well to inquire the best route and learn something about the building.
- Relax the night before the test – Allow your mind to rest. Do not study at all that night. Plan some mild recreation or diversion; then go to bed early and get a good night's sleep.
- Get up early enough to make a leisurely trip to the place for the test – This way unforeseen events, traffic snarls, unfamiliar buildings, etc. will not upset you.
- Dress comfortably – A written test is not a fashion show. You will be known by number and not by name, so wear something comfortable.

- Leave excess paraphernalia at home – Shopping bags and odd bundles will get in your way. You need bring only the items mentioned in the official notice you received; usually everything you need is provided. Do not bring reference books to the exam. They will only confuse those last minutes and be taken away from you when in the test room.
- Arrive somewhat ahead of time – If because of transportation schedules you must get there very early, bring a newspaper or magazine to take your mind off yourself while waiting.
- Locate the examination room – When you have found the proper room, you will be directed to the seat or part of the room where you will sit. Sometimes you are given a sheet of instructions to read while you are waiting. Do not fill out any forms until you are told to do so; just read them and be prepared.
- Relax and prepare to listen to the instructions
- If you have any physical problem that may keep you from doing your best, be sure to tell the test administrator. If you are sick or in poor health, you really cannot do your best on the exam. You can come back and take the test some other time.

VII. AT THE TEST

The day of the test is here and you have the test booklet in your hand. The temptation to get going is very strong. Caution! There is more to success than knowing the right answers. You must know how to identify your papers and understand variations in the type of short-answer question used in this particular examination. Follow these suggestions for maximum results from your efforts:

1) Cooperate with the monitor

The test administrator has a duty to create a situation in which you can be as much at ease as possible. He will give instructions, tell you when to begin, check to see that you are marking your answer sheet correctly, and so on. He is not there to guard you, although he will see that your competitors do not take unfair advantage. He wants to help you do your best.

2) Listen to all instructions

Don't jump the gun! Wait until you understand all directions. In most civil service tests you get more time than you need to answer the questions. So don't be in a hurry. Read each word of instructions until you clearly understand the meaning. Study the examples, listen to all announcements and follow directions. Ask questions if you do not understand what to do.

3) Identify your papers

Civil service exams are usually identified by number only. You will be assigned a number; you must not put your name on your test papers. Be sure to copy your number correctly. Since more than one exam may be given, copy your exact examination title.

4) Plan your time

Unless you are told that a test is a "speed" or "rate of work" test, speed itself is usually not important. Time enough to answer all the questions will be provided, but this does not mean that you have all day. An overall time limit has been set. Divide the total time (in minutes) by the number of questions to determine the approximate time you have for each question.

5) Do not linger over difficult questions

If you come across a difficult question, mark it with a paper clip (useful to have along) and come back to it when you have been through the booklet. One caution if you do this – be sure to skip a number on your answer sheet as well. Check often to be sure that you have not lost your place and that you are marking in the row numbered the same as the question you are answering.

6) Read the questions

Be sure you know what the question asks! Many capable people are unsuccessful because they failed to *read* the questions correctly.

7) Answer all questions

Unless you have been instructed that a penalty will be deducted for incorrect answers, it is better to guess than to omit a question.

8) Speed tests

It is often better NOT to guess on speed tests. It has been found that on timed tests people are tempted to spend the last few seconds before time is called in marking answers at random – without even reading them – in the hope of picking up a few extra points. To discourage this practice, the instructions may warn you that your score will be "corrected" for guessing. That is, a penalty will be applied. The incorrect answers will be deducted from the correct ones, or some other penalty formula will be used.

9) Review your answers

If you finish before time is called, go back to the questions you guessed or omitted to give them further thought. Review other answers if you have time.

10) Return your test materials

If you are ready to leave before others have finished or time is called, take ALL your materials to the monitor and leave quietly. Never take any test material with you. The monitor can discover whose papers are not complete, and taking a test booklet may be grounds for disqualification.

VIII. EXAMINATION TECHNIQUES

1) Read the general instructions carefully. These are usually printed on the first page of the exam booklet. As a rule, these instructions refer to the timing of the examination; the fact that you should not start work until the signal and must stop work at a signal, etc. If there are any *special* instructions, such as a choice of questions to be answered, make sure that you note this instruction carefully.

2) When you are ready to start work on the examination, that is as soon as the signal has been given, read the instructions to each question booklet, underline any key words or phrases, such as *least, best, outline, describe* and the like. In this way you will tend to answer as requested rather than discover on reviewing your paper that you *listed without describing*, that you selected the *worst* choice rather than the *best* choice, etc.

3) If the examination is of the objective or multiple-choice type – that is, each question will also give a series of possible answers: A, B, C or D, and you are called upon to select the best answer and write the letter next to that answer on your answer paper – it is advisable to start answering each question in turn. There may be anywhere from 50 to 100 such questions in the three or four hours allotted and you can see how much time would be taken if you read through all the questions before beginning to answer any. Furthermore, if you come across a question or group of questions which you know would be difficult to answer, it would undoubtedly affect your handling of all the other questions.

4) If the examination is of the essay type and contains but a few questions, it is a moot point as to whether you should read all the questions before starting to answer any one. Of course, if you are given a choice – say five out of seven and the like – then it is essential to read all the questions so you can eliminate the two that are most difficult. If, however, you are asked to answer all the questions, there may be danger in trying to answer the easiest one first because you may find that you will spend too much time on it. The best technique is to answer the first question, then proceed to the second, etc.

5) Time your answers. Before the exam begins, write down the time it started, then add the time allowed for the examination and write down the time it must be completed, then divide the time available somewhat as follows:
    - If 3-1/2 hours are allowed, that would be 210 minutes. If you have 80 objective-type questions, that would be an average of 2-1/2 minutes per question. Allow yourself no more than 2 minutes per question, or a total of 160 minutes, which will permit about 50 minutes to review.
    - If for the time allotment of 210 minutes there are 7 essay questions to answer, that would average about 30 minutes a question. Give yourself only 25 minutes per question so that you have about 35 minutes to review.

6) The most important instruction is to *read each question* and make sure you know what is wanted. The second most important instruction is to *time yourself properly* so that you answer every question. The third most important instruction is to *answer every question*. Guess if you have to but include something for each question. Remember that you will receive no credit for a blank and will probably receive some credit if you write something in answer to an essay question. If you guess a letter – say "B" for a multiple-choice question – you may have guessed right. If you leave a blank as an answer to a multiple-choice question, the examiners may respect your feelings but it will not add a point to your score. Some exams may penalize you for wrong answers, so in such cases *only*, you may not want to guess unless you have some basis for your answer.

7) Suggestions
    a. Objective-type questions
        1. Examine the question booklet for proper sequence of pages and questions
        2. Read all instructions carefully
        3. Skip any question which seems too difficult; return to it after all other questions have been answered
        4. Apportion your time properly; do not spend too much time on any single question or group of questions

5. Note and underline key words – *all, most, fewest, least, best, worst, same, opposite,* etc.
6. Pay particular attention to negatives
7. Note unusual option, e.g., unduly long, short, complex, different or similar in content to the body of the question
8. Observe the use of "hedging" words – *probably, may, most likely,* etc.
9. Make sure that your answer is put next to the same number as the question
10. Do not second-guess unless you have good reason to believe the second answer is definitely more correct
11. Cross out original answer if you decide another answer is more accurate; do not erase until you are ready to hand your paper in
12. Answer all questions; guess unless instructed otherwise
13. Leave time for review

b. Essay questions
1. Read each question carefully
2. Determine exactly what is wanted. Underline key words or phrases.
3. Decide on outline or paragraph answer
4. Include many different points and elements unless asked to develop any one or two points or elements
5. Show impartiality by giving pros and cons unless directed to select one side only
6. Make and write down any assumptions you find necessary to answer the questions
7. Watch your English, grammar, punctuation and choice of words
8. Time your answers; don't crowd material

8) Answering the essay question

Most essay questions can be answered by framing the specific response around several key words or ideas. Here are a few such key words or ideas:

M's: manpower, materials, methods, money, management
P's: purpose, program, policy, plan, procedure, practice, problems, pitfalls, personnel, public relations

a. Six basic steps in handling problems:
1. Preliminary plan and background development
2. Collect information, data and facts
3. Analyze and interpret information, data and facts
4. Analyze and develop solutions as well as make recommendations
5. Prepare report and sell recommendations
6. Install recommendations and follow up effectiveness

b. Pitfalls to avoid
1. *Taking things for granted* – A statement of the situation does not necessarily imply that each of the elements is necessarily true; for example, a complaint may be invalid and biased so that all that can be taken for granted is that a complaint has been registered

2. *Considering only one side of a situation* – Wherever possible, indicate several alternatives and then point out the reasons you selected the best one
3. *Failing to indicate follow up* – Whenever your answer indicates action on your part, make certain that you will take proper follow-up action to see how successful your recommendations, procedures or actions turn out to be
4. *Taking too long in answering any single question* – Remember to time your answers properly

IX. AFTER THE TEST

Scoring procedures differ in detail among civil service jurisdictions although the general principles are the same. Whether the papers are hand-scored or graded by machine we have described, they are nearly always graded by number. That is, the person who marks the paper knows only the number – never the name – of the applicant. Not until all the papers have been graded will they be matched with names. If other tests, such as training and experience or oral interview ratings have been given, scores will be combined. Different parts of the examination usually have different weights. For example, the written test might count 60 percent of the final grade, and a rating of training and experience 40 percent. In many jurisdictions, veterans will have a certain number of points added to their grades.

After the final grade has been determined, the names are placed in grade order and an eligible list is established. There are various methods for resolving ties between those who get the same final grade – probably the most common is to place first the name of the person whose application was received first. Job offers are made from the eligible list in the order the names appear on it. You will be notified of your grade and your rank as soon as all these computations have been made. This will be done as rapidly as possible.

People who are found to meet the requirements in the announcement are called "eligibles." Their names are put on a list of eligible candidates. An eligible's chances of getting a job depend on how high he stands on this list and how fast agencies are filling jobs from the list.

When a job is to be filled from a list of eligibles, the agency asks for the names of people on the list of eligibles for that job. When the civil service commission receives this request, it sends to the agency the names of the three people highest on this list. Or, if the job to be filled has specialized requirements, the office sends the agency the names of the top three persons who meet these requirements from the general list.

The appointing officer makes a choice from among the three people whose names were sent to him. If the selected person accepts the appointment, the names of the others are put back on the list to be considered for future openings.

That is the rule in hiring from all kinds of eligible lists, whether they are for typist, carpenter, chemist, or something else. For every vacancy, the appointing officer has his choice of any one of the top three eligibles on the list. This explains why the person whose name is on top of the list sometimes does not get an appointment when some of the persons lower on the list do. If the appointing officer chooses the second or third eligible, the No. 1 eligible does not get a job at once, but stays on the list until he is appointed or the list is terminated.

X. HOW TO PASS THE INTERVIEW TEST

The examination for which you applied requires an oral interview test. You have already taken the written test and you are now being called for the interview test – the final part of the formal examination.

You may think that it is not possible to prepare for an interview test and that there are no procedures to follow during an interview. Our purpose is to point out some things you can do in advance that will help you and some good rules to follow and pitfalls to avoid while you are being interviewed.

What is an interview supposed to test?

The written examination is designed to test the technical knowledge and competence of the candidate; the oral is designed to evaluate intangible qualities, not readily measured otherwise, and to establish a list showing the relative fitness of each candidate – as measured against his competitors – for the position sought. Scoring is not on the basis of "right" and "wrong," but on a sliding scale of values ranging from "not passable" to "outstanding." As a matter of fact, it is possible to achieve a relatively low score without a single "incorrect" answer because of evident weakness in the qualities being measured.

Occasionally, an examination may consist entirely of an oral test – either an individual or a group oral. In such cases, information is sought concerning the technical knowledges and abilities of the candidate, since there has been no written examination for this purpose. More commonly, however, an oral test is used to supplement a written examination.

Who conducts interviews?

The composition of oral boards varies among different jurisdictions. In nearly all, a representative of the personnel department serves as chairman. One of the members of the board may be a representative of the department in which the candidate would work. In some cases, "outside experts" are used, and, frequently, a businessman or some other representative of the general public is asked to serve. Labor and management or other special groups may be represented. The aim is to secure the services of experts in the appropriate field.

However the board is composed, it is a good idea (and not at all improper or unethical) to ascertain in advance of the interview who the members are and what groups they represent. When you are introduced to them, you will have some idea of their backgrounds and interests, and at least you will not stutter and stammer over their names.

What should be done before the interview?

While knowledge about the board members is useful and takes some of the surprise element out of the interview, there is other preparation which is more substantive. It *is* possible to prepare for an oral interview – in several ways:

1) Keep a copy of your application and review it carefully before the interview

This may be the only document before the oral board, and the starting point of the interview. Know what education and experience you have listed there, and the sequence and dates of all of it. Sometimes the board will ask you to review the highlights of your experience for them; you should not have to hem and haw doing it.

2) Study the class specification and the examination announcement

Usually, the oral board has one or both of these to guide them. The qualities, characteristics or knowledges required by the position sought are stated in these documents. They offer valuable clues as to the nature of the oral interview. For example, if the job involves supervisory responsibilities, the announcement will usually indicate that knowledge of modern supervisory methods and the qualifications of the candidate as a supervisor will be tested. If so, you can expect such questions, frequently in the form of a hypothetical situation which you are expected to solve. NEVER go into an oral without knowledge of the duties and responsibilities of the job you seek.

3) Think through each qualification required

Try to visualize the kind of questions you would ask if you were a board member. How well could you answer them? Try especially to appraise your own knowledge and background in each area, *measured against the job sought*, and identify any areas in which you are weak. Be critical and realistic – do not flatter yourself.

4) Do some general reading in areas in which you feel you may be weak

For example, if the job involves supervision and your past experience has NOT, some general reading in supervisory methods and practices, particularly in the field of human relations, might be useful. Do NOT study agency procedures or detailed manuals. The oral board will be testing your understanding and capacity, not your memory.

5) Get a good night's sleep and watch your general health and mental attitude

You will want a clear head at the interview. Take care of a cold or any other minor ailment, and of course, no hangovers.

What should be done on the day of the interview?

Now comes the day of the interview itself. Give yourself plenty of time to get there. Plan to arrive somewhat ahead of the scheduled time, particularly if your appointment is in the fore part of the day. If a previous candidate fails to appear, the board might be ready for you a bit early. By early afternoon an oral board is almost invariably behind schedule if there are many candidates, and you may have to wait. Take along a book or magazine to read, or your application to review, but leave any extraneous material in the waiting room when you go in for your interview. In any event, relax and compose yourself.

The matter of dress is important. The board is forming impressions about you – from your experience, your manners, your attitude, and your appearance. Give your personal appearance careful attention. Dress your best, but not your flashiest. Choose conservative, appropriate clothing, and be sure it is immaculate. This is a business interview, and your appearance should indicate that you regard it as such. Besides, being well groomed and properly dressed will help boost your confidence.

Sooner or later, someone will call your name and escort you into the interview room. *This is it.* From here on you are on your own. It is too late for any more preparation. But remember, you asked for this opportunity to prove your fitness, and you are here because your request was granted.

What happens when you go in?

The usual sequence of events will be as follows: The clerk (who is often the board stenographer) will introduce you to the chairman of the oral board, who will introduce you to the other members of the board. Acknowledge the introductions before you sit down. Do not be surprised if you find a microphone facing you or a stenotypist sitting by. Oral interviews are usually recorded in the event of an appeal or other review.

Usually the chairman of the board will open the interview by reviewing the highlights of your education and work experience from your application – primarily for the benefit of the other members of the board, as well as to get the material into the record. Do not interrupt or comment unless there is an error or significant misinterpretation; if that is the case, do not hesitate. But do not quibble about insignificant matters. Also, he will usually ask you some question about your education, experience or your present job – partly to get you to start talking and to establish the interviewing "rapport." He may start the actual questioning, or turn it over to one of the other members. Frequently, each member undertakes the questioning on a particular area, one in which he is perhaps most competent, so you can expect each member to participate in the examination. Because time is limited, you may also expect some rather abrupt switches in the direction the questioning takes, so do not be upset by it. Normally, a board member will not pursue a single line of questioning unless he discovers a particular strength or weakness.

After each member has participated, the chairman will usually ask whether any member has any further questions, then will ask you if you have anything you wish to add. Unless you are expecting this question, it may floor you. Worse, it may start you off on an extended, extemporaneous speech. The board is not usually seeking more information. The question is principally to offer you a last opportunity to present further qualifications or to indicate that you have nothing to add. So, if you feel that a significant qualification or characteristic has been overlooked, it is proper to point it out in a sentence or so. Do not compliment the board on the thoroughness of their examination – they have been sketchy, and you know it. If you wish, merely say, "No thank you, I have nothing further to add." This is a point where you can "talk yourself out" of a good impression or fail to present an important bit of information. Remember, *you close the interview yourself*.

The chairman will then say, "That is all, Mr. _____, thank you." Do not be startled; the interview is over, and quicker than you think. Thank him, gather your belongings and take your leave. Save your sigh of relief for the other side of the door.

How to put your best foot forward

Throughout this entire process, you may feel that the board individually and collectively is trying to pierce your defenses, seek out your hidden weaknesses and embarrass and confuse you. Actually, this is not true. They are obliged to make an appraisal of your qualifications for the job you are seeking, and they want to see you in your best light. Remember, they must interview all candidates and a non-cooperative candidate may become a failure in spite of their best efforts to bring out his qualifications. Here are 15 suggestions that will help you:

1) **Be natural – Keep your attitude confident, not cocky**

If you are not confident that you can do the job, do not expect the board to be. Do not apologize for your weaknesses, try to bring out your strong points. The board is interested in a positive, not negative, presentation. Cockiness will antagonize any board member and make him wonder if you are covering up a weakness by a false show of strength.

2) **Get comfortable, but don't lounge or sprawl**

Sit erectly but not stiffly. A careless posture may lead the board to conclude that you are careless in other things, or at least that you are not impressed by the importance of the occasion. Either conclusion is natural, even if incorrect. Do not fuss with your clothing, a pencil or an ashtray. Your hands may occasionally be useful to emphasize a point; do not let them become a point of distraction.

3) **Do not wisecrack or make small talk**

This is a serious situation, and your attitude should show that you consider it as such. Further, the time of the board is limited – they do not want to waste it, and neither should you.

4) Do not exaggerate your experience or abilities

In the first place, from information in the application or other interviews and sources, the board may know more about you than you think. Secondly, you probably will not get away with it. An experienced board is rather adept at spotting such a situation, so do not take the chance.

5) If you know a board member, do not make a point of it, yet do not hide it

Certainly you are not fooling him, and probably not the other members of the board. Do not try to take advantage of your acquaintanceship – it will probably do you little good.

6) Do not dominate the interview

Let the board do that. They will give you the clues – do not assume that you have to do all the talking. Realize that the board has a number of questions to ask you, and do not try to take up all the interview time by showing off your extensive knowledge of the answer to the first one.

7) Be attentive

You only have 20 minutes or so, and you should keep your attention at its sharpest throughout. When a member is addressing a problem or question to you, give him your undivided attention. Address your reply principally to him, but do not exclude the other board members.

8) Do not interrupt

A board member may be stating a problem for you to analyze. He will ask you a question when the time comes. Let him state the problem, and wait for the question.

9) Make sure you understand the question

Do not try to answer until you are sure what the question is. If it is not clear, restate it in your own words or ask the board member to clarify it for you. However, do not haggle about minor elements.

10) Reply promptly but not hastily

A common entry on oral board rating sheets is "candidate responded readily," or "candidate hesitated in replies." Respond as promptly and quickly as you can, but do not jump to a hasty, ill-considered answer.

11) Do not be peremptory in your answers

A brief answer is proper – but do not fire your answer back. That is a losing game from your point of view. The board member can probably ask questions much faster than you can answer them.

12) Do not try to create the answer you think the board member wants

He is interested in what kind of mind you have and how it works – not in playing games. Furthermore, he can usually spot this practice and will actually grade you down on it.

13) Do not switch sides in your reply merely to agree with a board member

Frequently, a member will take a contrary position merely to draw you out and to see if you are willing and able to defend your point of view. Do not start a debate, yet do not surrender a good position. If a position is worth taking, it is worth defending.

14) Do not be afraid to admit an error in judgment if you are shown to be wrong

The board knows that you are forced to reply without any opportunity for careful consideration. Your answer may be demonstrably wrong. If so, admit it and get on with the interview.

15) Do not dwell at length on your present job

The opening question may relate to your present assignment. Answer the question but do not go into an extended discussion. You are being examined for a *new* job, not your present one. As a matter of fact, try to phrase ALL your answers in terms of the job for which you are being examined.

Basis of Rating

Probably you will forget most of these "do's" and "don'ts" when you walk into the oral interview room. Even remembering them all will not ensure you a passing grade. Perhaps you did not have the qualifications in the first place. But remembering them will help you to put your best foot forward, without treading on the toes of the board members.

Rumor and popular opinion to the contrary notwithstanding, an oral board wants you to make the best appearance possible. They know you are under pressure – but they also want to see how you respond to it as a guide to what your reaction would be under the pressures of the job you seek. They will be influenced by the degree of poise you display, the personal traits you show and the manner in which you respond.

ABOUT THIS BOOK

This book contains tests divided into Examination Sections. Go through each test, answering every question in the margin. We have also attached a sample answer sheet at the back of the book that can be removed and used. At the end of each test look at the answer key and check your answers. On the ones you got wrong, look at the right answer choice and learn. Do not fill in the answers first. Do not memorize the questions and answers, but understand the answer and principles involved. On your test, the questions will likely be different from the samples. Questions are changed and new ones added. If you understand these past questions you should have success with any changes that arise. Tests may consist of several types of questions. We have additional books on each subject should more study be advisable or necessary for you. Finally, the more you study, the better prepared you will be. This book is intended to be the last thing you study before you walk into the examination room. Prior study of relevant texts is also recommended. NLC publishes some of these in our Fundamental Series. Knowledge and good sense are important factors in passing your exam. Good luck also helps. So now study this Passbook, absorb the material contained within and take that knowledge into the examination. Then do your best to pass that exam.

EXAMINATION SECTION

EXAMINATION SECTION
TEST 1

DIRECTIONS: Each question or incomplete statement is followed by several suggested answers or completions. Select the one that BEST answers the question or completes the statement. *PRINT THE LETTER OF THE CORRECT ANSWER IN THE SPACE AT THE RIGHT.*

1. A multi-line telephone with buttons for eight separate lines, plus a *hold* button, is often used when an office requires more than one outside line.
   If you are talking on one line of this type of office phone when another call comes in, what is the procedure to follow if you want to answer the second call but keep the first call on the line?
   Push the
   A. *hold* button at the same time as you push the *pickup* button of the ringing line
   B. *hold* button and then push the *pickup* button of the ringing line
   C. *pickup* button of the ringing line and then push the *hold* button
   D. *pickup* button of the ringing line and push the *hold* button when you return to the original line

   1.____

2. Suppose that you are asked to prepare a petty cash statement for March. The original and one copy are to go to the personnel office. One copy is to go to the fiscal office, and another copy is to go to your supervisor. The last copy is for your files.
   In preparing the statement and the copies, how many sheets of copy paper should you use?
   A. 3   B. 4   C. 5   D. 8

   2.____

3. Which one of the following is the LEAST important advantage of putting the subject of a letter in the heading to the right of the address? It
   A. makes filing of the copy easier
   B. makes more space available in the body of the letter
   C. simplifies distribution of letters
   D. simplifies determination of the subject of the letter

   3.____

4. Of the following, the MOST efficient way to put 100 copies of a one-page letter into 9½" x 4⅛" envelopes for mailing is to fold _____ into an envelope.
   A. each letter and insert it immediately after folding
   B. each letter separately until all 100 are folded; then insert each one
   C. the 100 letters two at a time, then separate them and insert each one
   D. two letters together, slip them apart, and insert each one

   4.____

5. When preparing papers for filing, it is NOT desirable to
   A. smooth papers that are wrinkled
   B. use paper clips to keep related papers together in the files
   C. arrange the papers in the order in which they will be filed
   D. mend torn papers with cellophane tape

6. Of the following, the BEST reason for a clerical unit to have its own duplicating machine is that the unit
   A. uses many forms which it must reproduce internally
   B. must make two copies of each piece of incoming mail for a special file
   C. must make seven copies of each piece of outgoing mail
   D. must type 200 envelopes each month for distribution to the same offices

7. Several offices use the same photocopying machine.
   If each office must pay its share of the cost of running this machine, the BEST way of determining how much of this cost should be charged to each of these offices is to
   A. determine the monthly number of photocopies made by each office
   B. determine the monthly number of originals submitted for photocopying by each office
   C. determine the number of times per day each office uses the photocopying machine
   D. divide the total cost of running the photocopy machine by the total number of offices using the machine

8. Which one of the following would it be BEST to use to indicate that a file folder has been removed from the files for temporary use in another office?
   A(n)
   A. cross-reference card   B. tickler file marker
   C. aperture card   D. out guide

9. Which one of the following is the MOST important objective of filing?
   A. Giving a secretary something to do in her spare time
   B. Making it possible to locate information quickly
   C. Providing a place to store unneeded documents
   D. Keeping extra papers from accumulating on workers' desks

10. If a check has been made out for an incorrect amount, the BEST action for the writer of the check to take is to
    A. erase the original amount and enter the correct amount
    B. cross out the original amount with a single line and enter the correct amount above it
    C. black out the original amount so that it cannot be read and enter the correct amount above it
    D. write a new check

11. Which one of the following BEST describes the usual arrangement of a tickler file?
    A. Alphabetical B. Chronological
    C. Numerical D. Geographical

12. Which one of the following is the LEAST desirable filing practice?
    A. Using staples to keep papers together
    B. Filing all material without regard to date
    C. Keeping a record of all materials removed from the files
    D. Writing filing instructions on each paper prior to filing

13. Assume that one of your duties is to keep records of the office supplies used by your unit for the purpose of ordering new supplies when the old supplies run out.
    The information that will be of MOST help in letting you know when to reorder supplies is the
    A. quantity issued B. quantity received
    C. quantity on hand D. stock number

Questions 14-19.

DIRECTIONS: Questions 14 through 19 consist of sets of names and addresses. In each question, the name and address in Column II should be an exact copy of the name and address in Column I. If there is
a mistake *only* in the name, mark your answer A;
a mistake *only* in the address, mark your answer B;
a mistake in *both* name and address, mark your answer C;
no mistake in either name or address, mark your answer D.

SAMPLE QUESTION

Column I
Michael Filbert
456 Reade Street
New York, N.Y. 10013

Column II
Michael Filbert
645 Reade Street
New York, N.Y. 10013

Since there is a mistake only in the address (the street number should be 456 instead of 645), the answer to the sample question is B.

COLUMN I

COLUMN II

14. Esta Wong
    141 West 68 St.
    New York, N.Y. 10023

    Esta Wang
    141 West 68 St.
    New York,, N.Y. 10023

15. Dr. Alberto Grosso
    3475 12th Avenue
    Brooklyn, N.Y. 11218

    Dr. Alberto Grosso
    3475 12th Avenue
    Brooklyn, N.Y. 11218

	Column I	Column II	
16.	Mrs. Ruth Bortlas 482 Theresa Ct. Far Rockaway, N.Y. 11691	Ms. Ruth Bortlas 482 Theresa Ct. Far Rockaway, N.Y. 11169	16.____
17.	Mr. and Mrs. Howard Fox 2301 Sedgwick Avenue Bronx, N.Y. 10468	Mr. and Mrs. Howard Fox 231 Sedgwick Ave. Bronx, N.Y. 10458	17.____
18.	Miss Marjorie Black 223 East 23 Street New York, N.Y. 10010	Miss Margorie Black 223 East 23 Street New York, N.Y. 10010	18.____
19.	Michelle Herman 806 Valley Rd. Old Tappan, N.J. 07675	Michelle Hermann 806 Valley Dr. Old Tappan, N.J. 07675	19.____

Questions 20-25.

DIRECTIONS: Questions 20 through 25 are to be answered SOLELY on the basis of the information in the following passage.

Basic to every office is the need for proper lighting. Inadequate lighting is a familiar cause of fatigue and serves to create a somewhat dismal atmosphere in the office. One requirement of proper lighting is that it be of an appropriate intensity. Intensity is measured in foot-candles. According to the Illuminating Engineering Society of New York, for casual seeing tasks such as in reception rooms, inactive file rooms, and other service areas, it is recommended that the amount of light be 30 foot-candles. For ordinary seeing tasks such as reading and work in active file rooms and in mail rooms, the recommended lighting is 100 foot-candles. For very difficult seeing tasks such as accounting, transcribing, and business machine use, the recommended lighting is 150 foot-candles.

Lighting intensity is only one requirement. Shadows and glare are to be avoided. For example, the larger the proportion of a ceiling filled with lighting units, the more glare-free and comfortable the lighting will be. Natural lighting from windows is not too dependable because on dark wintry days, windows yield little usable light, and on sunny afternoons, the glare from windows may be very distracting. Desks should not face the windows. Finally, the main lighting source ought to be overhead and to the left of the user.

20. According to the above passage, insufficient light in the office may cause 20.____
    A. glare   B. shadows   C. tiredness   D. distraction

21. Based on the above passage, which of the following must be considered when planning lighting arrangements? 21.____
    The
    A. amount of natural light present
    B. amount of work to be done
    C. level of difficulty of work to be done
    D. type of activity to be carried out

22. It can be inferred from the above passage that a well-coordinated lighting scheme is LIKELY to result in
    A. greater employee productivity
    B. elimination of light reflection
    C. lower lighting cost
    D. more use of natural light

23. Of the following, the BEST title for the above passage is
    A. Characteristics of Light
    B. Light Measurement Devices
    C. Factors to Consider When Planning Lighting Systems
    D. Comfort vs. Cost When Devising Lighting Arrangements

24. According to the above passage, a foot-candle is a measurement of the
    A. number of bulbs used
    B. strength of the light
    C. contrast between glare and shadow
    D. proportion of the ceiling filled with lighting units

25. According to the above passage, the number of foot-candles of light that would be needed to copy figures onto a payroll is _____ foot-candles.
    A. less than 30   B. 30   C. 100   D. 150

KEY (CORRECT ANSWERS)

1.	B		11.	B
2.	B		12.	B
3.	B		13.	C
4.	A		14.	A
5.	B		15.	D
6.	A		16.	C
7.	A		17.	B
8.	D		18.	A
9.	B		19.	C
10.	D		20.	C

21. D
22. A
23. C
24. B
25. D

TEST 2

DIRECTIONS: Each question or incomplete statement is followed by several suggested answers or completions. Select the one that BEST answers the question or completes the statement. *PRINT THE LETTER OF THE CORRECT ANSWER IN THE SPACE AT THE RIGHT.*

1. Assume that a supervisor has three subordinates who perform clerical tasks. One of the employees retires and is replaced by someone who is transferred from another unit in the agency. The transferred employee tells the supervisor that she has worked as a clerical employee for two years and understands clerical operations quite well. The supervisor then assigns the transferred employee to a desk, tells the employee to begin working, and returns to his own desk.
The supervisor's action in this situation is
   A. *proper;* experienced clerical employees do not require training when they are transferred to new assignments
   B. *improper;* before the supervisor returns to his desk, he should tell the other two subordinates to watch the transferred employee perform the work
   C. *proper;* if the transferred employee makes any mistakes, she will bring them to the supervisor's attention
   D. *improper;* the supervisor should find out what clerical tasks the transferred employee has performed and give her instruction in those which are new or different

1._____

2. Assume that you are falling behind in completing your work assignments and you believe that your workload is too heavy.
Of the following, the BEST course of action for you to take FIRST is to
   A. discuss the problem with your supervisor
   B. decide which of your assignments can be postponed
   C. try to get some of your co-workers to help you out
   D. plan to take some of the work home with you in order to catch up

2._____

3. Suppose that one of the clerks under your supervision is filling in monthly personnel forms. She asks you to explain a particular personnel regulation which is related to various items on the forms. You are not thoroughly familiar with the regulation.
Of the following responses you may make, the one which will gain the MOST respect from the clerk and which is generally the MOST advisable is to
   A. tell the clerk to do the best she can and that you will check her work later
   B. inform the clerk that you are not sure of a correct explanation but suggest a procedure for her to follow
   C. give the clerk a suitable interpretation so that she will think you are familiar with all regulations
   D. tell the clerk that you will have to read the regulation more thoroughly before you can give her an explanation

3._____

2 (#2)

4. Charging out records until a specified due date, with prompt follow-up if they are not returned, is a 4.____
   A. *good* idea; it may prevent the records from being kept needlessly on someone's desk for long periods of time
   B. *good* idea; it will indicate the extent of your authority to other departments
   C. *poor* idea; the person borrowing the material may make an error because of the pressure put upon him to return the records
   D. *poor* idea; other departments will feel that you do not trust them with the records and they will be resentful

Questions 5-9.

DIRECTIONS: Questions 5 through 9 consist of three lines of code letters and numbers. The numbers on each line should correspond with the code letters on the same line in accordance with the table below.

Code Letter	P	L	I	J	B	O	H	U	C	G
Corresponding Letter	0	1	2	3	4	5	6	7	8	9

On some of the lines, an error exists in the coding. Compare the letters and numbers in each question carefully. If you find an error or errors on
   only one of the lines in the question, mark your answer A;
   any two lines in the question, mark your answer B;
   all three lines in the question, mark your answer C;
   none of the lines in the question, mark your answer D.

SAMPLE QUESTION
JHOILCP   3652180
BICLGUP   4286970
UCIBHLJ   5824613

In the above sample, the first line is correct since each code letter listed has the correct corresponding number. On the second line, an error exists because code letter L should have the number 1 instead of the number 6. On the third line, an error exists because the code letter U should have the number 7 instead of the number 5. Since there are errors on two of the three lines, the correct answer is B.

5. BULJCIP   4713920   5.____
    HIGPOUL   6290571
    OCUHJJBI   5876342

6. CUBLOIJ   8741023   6.____
    LCLGCLB   1818914
    JPUHIOC   3076158

7. OIJGCBPO   52398405   7.____
    UHPBLIOP   76041250
    CLUIPGPC   81720908

7

3 (#2)

8. BPCOUOJI   40875732   8._____
    UOHCIPLB   75682014
    GLHUUCBJ   92677843

9. HOIOHJLH   65256361   9._____
    IOJJHHBP   25536640
    OJHBJOPI   53642502

Questions 10-13.

DIRECTIONS: Questions 10 through 13 are to be answered SOLELY on the basis of the information given in the following passage.

The mental attitude of the employee toward safety is exceedingly important in preventing accidents. All efforts designed to keep safety on the employee's mind and to keep accident prevention a live subject in the office will help substantially in a safety program. Although it may seem strange, it is common for people to be careless. Therefore, safety education is a continuous process.

Safety rules should be explained, and the reasons for their rigid enforcement should be given to employees. Telling employees to be careful or giving similar general safety warnings and slogans is probably of little value. Employees should be informed of basic safety fundamentals. This can be done through staff meetings, informal suggestions to employees, movies, and safety instruction cards. Safety instruction cards provide the employees with specific suggestions about safety and serve as a series of timely reminder helping to keep safety on the minds of employees. Pictures, posters, and cartoon sketches on bulletin boards that are located in areas continually used by employees arouse the employees' interest in safety. It is usually good to supplement this type of safety promotion with intensive individual follow-up.

10. The above passage implies that the LEAST effective of the following safety   10._____
    measures is
    A. rigid enforcement of safety rules
    B. getting employees to think in terms of safety
    C. elimination of unsafe conditions in the office
    D. telling employees to stay alert at all times

11. The reason given by the passage for maintaining ongoing safety education is   11._____
    that
    A. people are often careless
    B. office tasks are often dangerous
    C. the value of safety slogans increases with repetition
    D. safety rules change frequently

12. Which one of the following safety aids is MOST likely to be preferred by the   12._____
    passage? A
    A. cartoon of a man tripping over a carton and yelling, *Keep aisles clear!*
    B. poster with a large number one and a caption saying, *Safety First*

C. photograph of a very neatly arranged office
D. large sign with the word THINK in capital letters

13. Of the following, the BEST title for the above passage is   13.____
    A. Basic Safety Fundamentals
    B. Enforcing Safety Among Careless Employees
    C. Attitudes Toward Safety
    D. Making Employees Aware of Safety

Questions 14-21.

DIRECTIONS: Questions 14 through 21 are to be answered SOLELY on the basis of the information and chart given below.

The following chart shows expenses in five selected categories for a one-year period, expressed as percentages of these same expenses during the previous year. The chart compares two different offices. In Office T (represented by ▓▓▓▓), a cost reduction program has been tested for the past year. The other office, Office Q (represented by ▨▨▨▨), served as a control, in that no special effort was made to reduce costs during the past year.

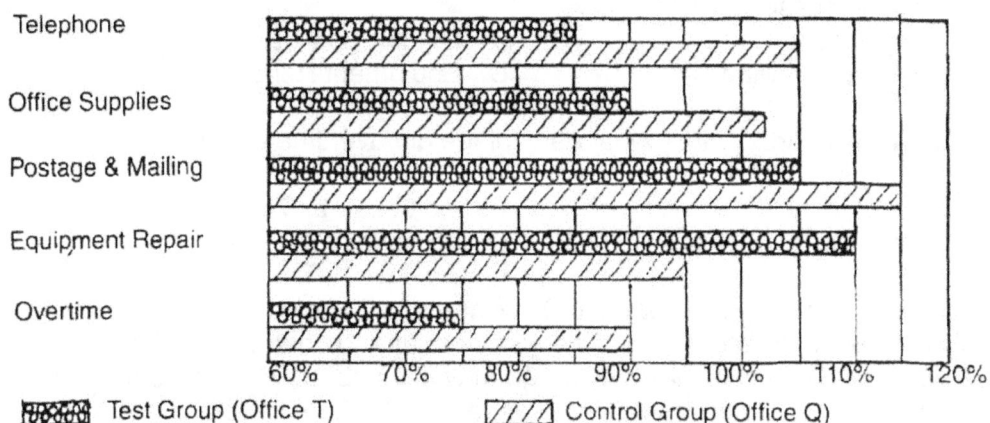

14. In Office T, which category of expense showed the greatest percentage   14.____
    REDUCTION from 2019 to 2020?
    A. Telephone   B. Office Supplies
    C. Postage & Mailing   D. Overtime

15. In which expense category did Office T show the BEST results in percentage   15.____
    terms when compared to Office Q?
    A. Telephone   B. Office Supplies
    C. Postage & Mailing   D. Overtime

16. According to the above chart, the cost reduction program was LEAST effective for the expense category of
    A. Office Supplies
    B. Postage & Mailing
    C. Equipment Repair
    D. Overtime

17. Office T's telephone costs went down during 2020 by approximately how many percentage points?
    A. 15   B. 20   C. 85   D. 104

18. Which of the following changes occurred in expenses for Office Supplies in Office Q in the year 2020 as compared with the year 2019?
    They
    A. increased by more than 100%
    B. remained the same
    C. decreased by a few percentage points
    D. increased by a few percentage points

19. For which of the following expense categories do the results in Office T and the results in Office Q differ MOST NEARLYY by 10 percentage points?
    A. Telephone
    B. Postage & Mailing
    C. Equipment Repair
    D. Overtime

20. In which expense category did Office Q's costs show the GREATEST percentage increase in 2020?
    A. Telephone
    B. Office Supplies
    C. Postage & Mailing
    D. Equipment Repair

21. In Office T, by approximately what percentage did overtime expense change during the past year? It
    A. *increased* by 15%
    B. *increased* by 75%
    C. *decreased* by 10%
    D. *decreased* by 25%

22. In a particular agency, there were 160 accidents in 2017. Of these accidents, 75% were due to unsafe acts and the rest were due to unsafe conditions. In the following year, a special safety program was established. The number of accidents in 2019 due to unsafe acts was reduced to 35% of what it had been in 2017.
    How many accidents due to unsafe acts were there in 2019?
    A. 20   B. 36   C. 42   D. 56

23. At the end of every month, the petty cash fund of Agency A is reimbursed for payments made from the fund during the month. During the month of February, the amounts paid from the fund were entered on receipts as follows: 10 bus fares of $3.50 each and one taxi fare of $35.00. At the end of the month, the money left in the fund was in the following denominations: 15 ten-dollar bills, 10 one-dollar bills, 40 quarters, and 100 dimes.
    If the petty cash fund is reduced by 20% for the following month, how much money will there be available in the petty cash fund for March?
    A. $110.00   B. $200.00   C. $215.00   D. $250.00

24. The one of the following records which it would be MOST advisable to keep in alphabetical order is a
    A. continuous listing of phone messages, including time and caller, for your supervisor
    B. listing of individuals currently employed by your agency in a particular title
    C. record of purchases paid for by the petty cash fund
    D. dated record of employees who have borrowed material from the files in your office

25. Assume that you have been asked to copy by hand a column of numbers with two decimal places from one record to another. Each number consists of three, four, and five digits.
    In order to copy them quickly and accurately, you should copy
    A. each number exactly, making sure that the column of digits farthest to the right is in a straight line and all other columns are lined up
    B. the column of digits farthest to the right and then copy the next column of digits moving from right to left
    C. the column of digits farthest to the left and then copy the next column of digits moving from left to right
    D. the digits to the right of each decimal point and then copy the digits to the left of each decimal point

KEY (CORRECT ANSWERS)

1.	D		11.	A
2.	A		12.	A
3.	D		13.	D
4.	A		14.	D
5.	A		15.	A
6.	C		16.	C
7.	D		17.	A
8.	B		18.	D
9.	C		19.	B
10.	D		20.	C

21.	D
22.	C
23.	B
24.	B
25.	A

EXAMINATION SECTION
TEST 1

DIRECTIONS: Each question or incomplete statement is followed by several suggested answers or completions. Select the one that BEST answers the question or completes the statement. *PRINT THE LETTER OF THE CORRECT ANSWER IN THE SPACE AT THE RIGHT.*

1. Assume that you have been assigned by your supervisor to file some record cards in a cabinet. All the cards in this cabinet are supposed to be kept in strict alphabetical order. You know that important work is being held up because certain cards in this cabinet cannot be located. While filing the records given you, you come across a card which is not in its correct alphabetical place.
   Of the following, the BEST reason for you to bring this record to the attention of your supervisor is that

   A. errors in filing are more serious than other types of errors
   B. your alertness in locating the card should be rewarded
   C. the filing system may be at fault, rather than the employee who misfiled the card
   D. time may be saved by such action

2. Assume that you are the receptionist for Mr. Brown, an official in your department. It is your duty to permit only persons having important business to see this official; otherwise, you are to refer them to other members of the staff. A man tells you that he must see Mr. Brown on a very urgent and confidential matter. He gives you his name and says that Mr. Brown knows him, but he does not wish to tell you the nature of the matter.
   Of the following, the BEST action for you to take under these circumstances is to

   A. permit this man to see Mr. Brown without further question since the matter seems to be urgent
   B. refer this man to another member of the staff, since Mr. Brown may not wish to see him
   C. call Mr. Brown and explain the situation to him, and ask him whether he wishes to see this man
   D. tell this man that you will permit him to see Mr. Brown only if he informs you of the nature of his business

3. You are given copies of an important official notice, together with a memorandum stating that each of the employees listed on the memorandum is to receive a copy of the official notice.
   In order to have definite proof that each of the employees listed has received a copy of the notice, the BEST of the following courses of action for you to take as you hand the notice to each of the employees is to

   A. put your initial next to the employee's name on the memorandum
   B. ask the employee to sign the notice you have given in your presence
   C. have the employee put his signature next to his name on the memorandum
   D. ask the employee to read the notice in your presence

4. Suppose that you are assigned to the information window of a city department where you come in daily contact with many people. On one occasion, a man asks you for some information in a very arrogant and rude manner.
Of the following, the BEST reason for you to give this man the requested information politely is that

   A. he may not mean to be rude; it may just be his manner of speech
   B. it is the duty of city employees to teach members of the public to be polite
   C. he will probably apologize for his manner when he sees that you are polite
   D. city employees are expected to be courteous to the public

5. Assume that you have been placed in charge of a stock room in a city department and that one of your duties is to take a periodic inventory of the supplies you have on hand.
Of the following, the BEST justification for this procedure is

   A. you will know which supplies are running low
   B. accurate records need not be kept in all stock rooms
   C. you will become more familiar with the location of the different items in the stock room
   D. it will prevent the needless waste of supplies by the employees of the department

6. It is an accepted practice to have the initials of the person who dictates a letter, as well as those of the person who types it, appear in the lower left-hand corner of the letter.
Of the following, the CHIEF justification for this procedure is that it

   A. may be used as a means of measuring output of work
   B. fixes responsibility
   C. aids in filing
   D. avoids the need for making carbon copies

7. Suppose that you are given several sheets containing an unalphabetized list of 500 names and a corresponding set of 500 disarranged cards. Your supervisor asks you to check to see that for every name on the list there is a corresponding card.
Of the following, the MOST efficient procedure for you to follow is to

   A. arrange both the cards and the names on the list in alphabetical order and check one against the other
   B. alphabetize the list only and check each card in turn against the names on the list
   C. alphabetize the cards only and check each name on the list in turn against the cards
   D. alphabetize neither the cards nor the list, but take each card in turn and find the corresponding name on the list

8. The clerk could not recall the name of the person to whom his supervisor had requested him to make a check payable. He therefore made it payable to *Cash*.
This action on the part of the clerk is

   A. to be praised; he showed ingenuity
   B. to be criticized; if lost, the check might be cashed by anyone finding it
   C. inexcusable; a check must be made payable to a definite person
   D. correct; in the future, he should make all checks payable to *Cash*

9. Assume that one of your duties as a clerk is to keep a constantly changing mailing list up-to-date.
   Of the following, the BEST method for you to follow is to use use a(n)

   A. alphabetical card index with loose cards, one for each name
   B. bound volume with a separate page or group of pages for each letter
   C. loose-leaf notebook with names beginning with the same letter listed on the same sheet or group of sheets
   D. typed list, add names at end of the list, and retype periodically in proper alphabetical order

10. In evaluating the effectiveness of a filing system, the one of the following criteria which you should consider MOST important is the

    A. safety of material in the event of a fire
    B. ease with which material may be located
    C. quantity of papers which can be filed
    D. extent to which material in the filing system is being used

11. A set of cards numbered from 1 to 300 has been filed in numerical order in such a way that the highest number is at the front of the file and the lowest number is at the rear. It is desired that the cards be reversed to run in ascending order.
    The BEST of the following methods that can be used in performing this task is to begin at the

    A. front of the file and remove the cards one at a time, placing each one face up on top of the one removed before
    B. front of the file and remove the cards one at a time, placing each one face down on top of the one removed before
    C. back of the file and remove the cards in small groups, placing each group face down on top of the group removed before
    D. back of the file and remove the cards one at a time, placing each one face up on top of the one removed before

12. A person would MOST likely make a *person-to-person* long distance telephone call when

    A. he does not know whether the person to whom he wishes to speak is in
    B. he wishes to speak to any person answering the telephone
    C. he knows that the person to whom he wishes to speak will answer the telephone
    D. the call is made before 7 P.M.

13. In a certain file room, it is customary, when removing a record from the files, to insert an *out* card in its place. A clerk suggests keeping, in addition, a chronological list of all records removed and the names of the employees who have removed them.
    This suggestion would be of GREATEST value

    A. in avoiding duplication of work
    B. in enabling an employee to refile records more easily
    C. where records are frequently misfiled
    D. where records are frequently kept out longer than necessary

14. You are given a large batch of correspondence and asked to obtain the folder on file for each of the senders of these letters. The folders in your file room are kept in numerical order and an alphabetic cross-index file is maintained.
    Of the following, the BEST procedure would be for you to

    A. look up the numbers in the alphabetic file, then alphabetize the correspondence according to the senders' names and obtain the folders from the numerical file
    B. alphabetize the correspondence according to the senders' names, get the file numbers from the alphabetic file, and obtain the folders from the numerical file
    C. alphabetize the correspondence and then look through the numerical file for the proper folders in the order in which your correspondence is arranged
    D. look through the numerical file, pulling out the folders as you come across them

14.____

15. Designing forms of the proper size is of the utmost importance. Certain sizes are best because they can be cut without waste from standard sheets of paper on which forms are printed and because they fit standard files and binders.
    The one of the following which is the MOST valid implication of the above passage is that

    A. the size of a form should be decided upon before the information is printed on it
    B. the size of a form should be such that it can be printed on paper without cutting
    C. the person designing a form should be acquainted with standard sizes in file cabinets and paper
    D. the purpose of a form is an important factor in the determination of its size

15.____

16. When an employee is encouraged by his supervisor to think of new ideas in connection with his work, the habit of improving work methods is fostered.
    The one of the following which is the MOST valid implication of the above statement is that

    A. the improvement of work methods should be the concern not only of the supervisor but of the employee as well
    B. an employee without initiative cannot perform his job well
    C. an employee may waste too much time in experimenting with new work methods
    D. an improved method for performing a task should not be used without the approval of the supervisor

16.____

17. The report on the work of the three employees furnishes definite proof that Jones is more efficient than Smith, and that Brown is less efficient than Jones.
    On the basis of the above information, the MOST accurate of the following statements is that

    A. Brown is more efficient than Smith
    B. Smith is more efficient than Brown
    C. Smith is not necessarily less efficient than Jones
    D. Brown is not necessarily more efficient than Smith

17.____

18. Almost all students with a high school average of 80% or over were admitted to the college.
    On the basis of this statement, it would be MOST accurate to assume that

18.____

A. a high school average of 80% or over was required for admittance to the college
B. some students with a high school average of less than 80% were admitted to the college
C. a high school average of at least 80% was desirable but not necessary for admission to the college
D. some students with a high school average of at least 80% were not admitted to the college

Questions 19-21.

DIRECTIONS: Questions 19 to 21 are to be answered SOLELY on the basis of the information contained in the following passage.

It is common knowledge that ability to do a particular job and performance on the job do not always go hand-in-hand. Persons with great potential abilities sometimes fall down on the job because of laziness or lack of interest in the job, while persons with mediocre talents have often achieved excellent results through their industry and their loyalty to the interests of their employers. It is clear, therefore, that in a balanced personnel program, measures of employee ability need to be supplemented by measures of employee performance, for the final test of any employee is his performance on the job.

19. The MOST accurate of the following statements, on the basis of the above paragraph, is that

    A. employees who lack ability are usually not industrious
    B. an employee's attitudes are more important than his abilities
    C. mediocre employees who are interested in their work are preferable to employees who possess great ability
    D. superior capacity for performance should be supplemented with proper attitudes

19.____

20. On the basis of the above paragraph, the employee of most value to his employer is NOT necessarily the one who

    A. best understands the significance of his duties
    B. achieves excellent results
    C. possesses the greatest talents
    D. produces the greatest amount of work

20.____

21. According to the above paragraph, an employee's efficiency is BEST determined by an

    A. appraisal of his interest in his work
    B. evaluation of the work performed by him
    C. appraisal of his loyalty to his employer
    D. evaluation of his potential ability to perform his work

21.____

22. Assume that you know the capacity of a filing cabinet, the extent of which it is filled, and the daily rate at which material is being added to the file.
In order to estimate how many more days it will take for the cabinet to be filled to capacity, you should

    A. divide the extent to which the cabinet is filled by the daily rate
    B. take the difference between the capacity of the cabinet and the material in it, and multiply the result by the daily rate of adding material

22.____

C. divide the daily rate of adding material by the difference between the capacity of the cabinet and the material in it
D. take the difference between the capacity of the cabinet and the material in it, and divide the result by the daily rate of adding material

23. Suppose you have been asked to compute the average salary earned in your department during the past year. For each of the divisions of the department, you are given the number of employees and the average salary.
In order to find the requested overall average salary for the department, you should

    A. add the average salaries of the various divisions and divide the total by the number of divisions
    B. multiply the number of employees in each division by the corresponding average salary, add the results and divide the total by the number of employees in the department
    C. add the average salaries of the various divisions and divide the total by the total number of employees in the department
    D. multiply the sum of the average salaries of the various divisions by the total number of divisions and divide the resulting product by the total number of employees in the department

24. Three divisions within a department are working to complete a major six-month project with varying levels of responsibility. A manager asks you to prepare a chart or graph that indicates each division's share (by percentage) of the project's total expenses to date for review by a department supervisor. The most effective type of chart or graph to use in this case would be a

    A. pie chart   B. line graph
    C. bar graph   D. Venn diagram

25. A study of the grades of students in a certain college revealed that in 2005, 15% fewer students received a passing grade in mathematics than in 2004, whereas in 2006, the number of students passing mathematics increased 15% over 2005.
On the basis of this study, it would be MOST accurate to conclude that

    A. the same percentage of students passed mathematics in 2004 as in 2006
    B. of the three years studied, the greatest percentage of students passed mathematics in 2006
    C. the percentage of students who passed mathematics in 2006 was less than the percentage passing this subject in 2004
    D. the percentage of students passing mathematics in 2004 was 15% greater than the percentage of students passing this subject in 2006

26. Some authority must determine finally whether constitutional guarantees mean literally and absolutely what they say, or something less or perchance more.
In the American system of government, that authority rests with the

    A. elected representatives in Congress
    B. executive branch of the federal government
    C. courts
    D. state legislatures

27. Almost all city departments obtain their supplies and equipment through the Department of Purchase.
Of the following, the CHIEF justification for this procedure is to effect savings by means of

    A. large-scale consumption of standard office supplies
    B. competitive bidding
    C. centralized buying
    D. non-profit purchasing

27.____

28. The one of the following federal agencies which is MOST concerned with the conservation of natural resources in this country is the

    A. Department of Interior
    B. Federal Trade Commission
    C. Department of Commerce
    D. Department of State

28.____

29. A city employee who is familiar with economic affairs should know that a period of inflation can BEST be characterized as a period when

    A. there is universal prosperity
    B. savings can buy fewer things than anticipated
    C. the cost of necessities is high and the cost of luxuries is low
    D. the value of money is increased

29.____

30. A clerk interested in world affairs should know that UNESCO is concerned MAINLY with international cooperation

    A. in the control of atomic power
    B. in the relocation of refugees
    C. to raise health standards throughout the world
    D. through the free exchange of information on education, art, and science

30.____

31. Suppose that your supervisor gives you a folder of approximately 200 letters, arranged chronologically, and a list of the names of the writers of these letters, arranged alphabetically. He asks you to verify, without disarranging the order of the letters, that there is a letter in the folder for each name on the list. Of the following, the BEST procedure for you to follow is to

    A. glance at each of the letters in the folder in turn and place a light pencil check on the alphabetical list next to the name of the person writing that letter
    B. glance at each of the letters in the folder in turn and place a light pencil check on each letter if there is a corresponding name on the alphabetical list
    C. rearrange the letters in alphabetical order and verify that there is a one-to-one relationship between letters and names
    D. rewrite the names on the list in chronological order and verify that there is a one-to-one relationship between letters and names

31.____

32. Suppose that you will not be able to complete today an important job that you have been assigned and that you expect to be out of the office the next few days.
In general, the BEST action for you to take before leaving the office at the end of the day is to

    A. apportion the remainder of your work equally among the other clerks in your office
    B. arrange your work neatly on top of your desk

32.____

C. tell your supervisor exactly how much of the work you have been able to do
D. lock your work in your desk so that your work cannot be disturbed in your absence

33. Suppose that your supervisor has asked you to make a copy of a statistical table. In general, the BEST method for checking the copy you prepare in order to make certain that the copy is absolutely accurate is for you to

A. make a second copy of the table and compare the two copies
B. have another clerk read the original table aloud to you while you read the copy
C. compare all totals in the two tables, for if the totals check, the copy is probably accurate
D. check the one or two points in the table at which an error is most likely to be made

34. Suppose that, in the course of your work, you frequently come into contact with the public.
The one of the following which is the BEST reason for courtesy in all your contacts with the public is that

A. most individuals are fully aware of the methods and procedures of city departments
B. some individuals who come to city agencies for information or assistance are so domineering in their attitude that it is difficult to be polite
C. no employee of a private business organization would dare to be discourteous to a customer
D. a favorable attitude on the part of the public toward civil service employees is necessary for maintenance of the merit system

35. *It is good office practice, when answering the telephone, to give immediately the name of the office in which you work.*
Of the following, the BEST reason for following this practice is that it

A. identifies immediately the particular person answering the telephone
B. avoids loss of time due to mistaken or uncertain identity
C. stimulates employees to answer the telephone quickly
D. indicates directly that your supervisor is not in the office

Questions 36-44.

DIRECTIONS: Questions 36 to 44 consist of 9 groups of names. Consider each group of names as a unit. Determine in what position the name printed in ITALICS would be if the names in the group were CORRECTLY arranged in alphabetical order. If the name in italics should be first, print the letter A; if second, print the letter B; if third, print the letter C; if fourth, print the letter D; and if fifth, print the letter E. Indicate the answer in the space at the right. Below are some rules for alphabetizing which you are to use as a guide in answering these items:

1. Arrange alphabetically, first, according to surnames; when surnames are the same, then according to given names or initials; when given names or initials are also the same, then according to middle names or initials.
2. An initial precedes a name beginning with the same letter. For example: J. Martin precedes James Martin.

3. A name without a middle name or initial precedes the same name having a middle name or initial.
   For example: James Martin precedes James E. Martin.
4. Treat all abbreviations as if spelled out in full when the names for which they stand are commonly understood.
5. Arrange names beginning with "Mc" or "Mac" in their exact alphabetic order as spelled.
6. Treat names containing numerals as if numerals were spelled out.
7. The names of business organizations which do not include the name of a person are alphabetized as written, subject to the provisions of Rule 8.
8. Disregard the following in alphabetizing: <u>the</u>, <u>and</u>, titles and designations as <u>Dr</u>., <u>Mr</u>., <u>Mrs</u>., <u>Jr</u>., and Sr.

SAMPLE ITEM:
   J.W. Martin   (2)
   James E. Martin (4)
   J. Martin   (1)
   George Martins   (5)
   James Martin   (3)

The correct alphabetic order is indicated alongside the names in the sample item, and the correct answer should be D.

36. Albert Brown
    James Borenstein
    Frieda Albrecht
    Samuel Brown
    George Appelman

36.____

37. James Ryn
    Francis Ryan
    Wm. Roanan
    Frances S. Ryan
    Francis P. Ryan

37.____

38. Norman Fitzgibbons
    Charles F. Franklin
    Jas. Fitzgerald
    Andrew Fitzsimmons
    James P. Fitzgerald

38.____

39. Hugh F. Martenson
    A.S. Martinson
    Albert Martinsen
    Albert S. Martinson
    M. Martanson

39.____

40. Aaron M. Michelson
    Samuel Michels
    Arthur L. Michaelson, Sr.
    John Michell
    Daniel Michelsohn

40.____

41. *Chas. R. Connolly*
    Frank Conlon
    Charles S. Connolly
    Abraham Cohen
    Chas. Conolly

41.____

42. James McCormack
    Ruth MacNamara
    Kathryn McGillicuddy
    Frances Mason
    Arthur MacAdams

42.____

43. Dr. Francis Karell
    John Joseph Karelsen, jr.
    John J. Karelsen, Sr.
    Mrs. Jeanette Kelly
    Estelle Karel

43.____

44. *The 5th Ave. Bus Co.*
    The Baltimore and Ohio Railroad
    3rd Ave. Elevated Co.
    The 4th Ave. Trolley Line

44.____

Questions 45-53.

DIRECTIONS: The following table contains certain information about employees in a city bureau. Questions 45 to 53 are to be answered on the basis of the facts given in this table.

RECORD OF EMPLOYEES IN A CITY BUREAU

NAME	TITLE	AGE	ANNUAL SALARY	YEARS OF SERVICE	EXAMINATION RATING
Jones	Clerk	34	$20,400	10	82
Smith	Stenographer	25	19,200	2	72
Black	Typist	19	14,400	1	71
Brown	Stenographer	36	25,200	12	88
Thomas	Accountant	49	41,200	21	91
Gordon	Clerk	31	30,000	8	81
Johnson	Stenographer	26	26,400	5	75
White	Accountant	53	36,000	30	90
Spencer	Clerk	42	27,600	19	85
Taylor	Typist	24	21,600	5	74
Simpson	Accountant	37	50,000	11	87
Reid	Typist	20	12,000	2	72
Fulton	Accountant	55	55,000	31	100
Chambers	Clerk	22	15,600	4	75
Calhoun	Stenographer	48	28,800	16	80

45. The name of the employee whose salary would be the middle one if all the salaries were ranked in order of magnitude is   45._____

    A. White   B. Johnson   C. Brown   D. Spencer

46. The combined monthly salary of all the stenographers exceeds the combined monthly salary of all the clerks by   46._____

    A. $6,000   B. $500   C. $22,800   D. $600

47. The age of the employee who received the HIGHEST rating in the examination among those who have less than 10 years of service is _____ years.   47._____

    A. 22   B. 31   C. 55   D. 34

48. The average examination rating of those employees who had 15 years of service or more as compared with the average examination rating of those employees who had 5 years of service or less is MOST NEARLY   48._____

    A. 16 points greater   B. 7 points greater
    C. 10 points less   D. 25 points greater

49. The name of the youngest employee whose monthly salary is more than $1,000 per month and who has more than one year of service is   49._____

    A. Reid   B. Black   C. Chambers   D. Taylor

50. The name of the employee who received an examination rating of over 85%, who has more than 15 years of service, and who earns a yearly salary of more than $25,000 but less than $40,000 is   50._____

    A. Thomas   B. Spencer   C. Calhoun   D. White

KEY (CORRECT ANSWERS)

1. D	11. A	21. B	31. A	41. C
2. C	12. A	22. D	32. C	42. C
3. C	13. D	23. B	33. B	43. D
4. D	14. B	24. A	34. D	44. B
5. A	15. C	25. A	35. B	45. B
6. B	16. A	26. C	36. E	46. B
7. C	17. D	27. C	37. D	47. B
8. B	18. D	28. A	38. A	48. A
9. A	19. D	29. B	39. E	49. C
10. B	20. C	30. D	40. D	50. D

TEST 2

DIRECTIONS: Each question or incomplete statement is followed by several suggested answers or completions. Select the one that BEST answers the question or completes the statement. *PRINT THE LETTER OF THE CORRECT ANSWER IN THE SPACE AT THE RIGHT.*

1. The annual salary of the HIGHEST paid stenographer is

   A. more than twice as great as the salary of the youngest employee
   B. greater than the salary of the oldest typist but not as great as the salary of the oldest clerk
   C. greater than the salary of the highest paid typist but not as great as the salary of the lowest paid accountant
   D. less than the combined salaries of the two youngest typists

2. The number of employees whose annual salary is more than $15,600 but less than $28,800 and who have at least 5 years of service is

   A. 11   B. 8   C. 6   D. 5

3. Of the following, it would be MOST accurate to state that the

   A. youngest employee is lowest with respect to number of years of service, examination rating, and salary
   B. oldest employee is highest with respect to number of years of service, examination rating, but not with respect to salary
   C. annual salary of the youngest clerk is $1,200 more than the annual salary of the youngest typist and $2,400 less than the annual salary of the youngest stenographer
   D. difference in age between the youngest and oldest typist is less than one-fourth the difference in age between the youngest and oldest stenographer

4. *He advocated a new course of action.* The word *advocated* means MOST NEARLY

   A. described   B. refused to discuss
   C. argued against   D. supported

5. A clerk who is assigned to make a *facsimile* of a report should make a copy which is

   A. exact   B. larger   C. smaller   D. edited

6. *A city employee must be a person of integrity.* The word *integrity* means MOST NEARLY

   A. intelligence   B. competence
   C. honesty   D. keenness

7. A person who displays *apathy* is

   A. irritated   B. confused
   C. indifferent   D. insubordinate

8. *The supervisor admonished the clerk for his tardiness.* The word *admonished* means MOST NEARLY

   A. reproved   B. excused   C. transferred   D. punished

9. A *lucrative* business is one which is

   A. unprofitable B. gainful C. unlawful D. speculative

10. To say that the work is *tedious* means MOST NEARLY that it is

    A. technical
    C. tiresome
    B. interesting
    D. confidential

11. A *vivacious* person is one who is

    A. kind B. talkative C. lively D. well-dressed

12. An *innocuous* statement is one which is

    A. forceful B. harmless C. offensive D. brief

13. To say that the order was *rescinded* means MOST NEARLY that it was

    A. revised
    C. misinterpreted
    B. canceled
    D. confirmed

14. To say that the administrator *amplified* his remarks means MOST NEARLY that the remarks were

    A. shouted
    C. carefully analyzed
    B. expanded
    D. summarized briefly

15. *Peremptory* commands will be resented in any office. The word *peremptory* means MOST NEARLY

    A. unexpected
    C. military
    B. unreasonable
    D. dictatorial

16. A clerk should know that the word *sporadic* means MOST NEARLY

    A. occurring regularly
    C. scattered
    B. sudden
    D. disturbing

17. To *vacillate* means MOST NEARLY to

    A. lubricate B. waver C. decide D. investigate

18. A *homogeneous* group of persons is characterized by its

    A. similarity
    C. discontent
    B. teamwork
    D. differences

19. A *vindictive* person is one who is

    A. prejudiced B. unpopular C. petty D. revengeful

20. The abbreviation *e.g.* occurs frequently in written matter and is commonly taken to mean

    A. note carefully
    C. entire group
    B. for example
    D. and others

21. The abbreviation *i.e.* also occurs frequently in written matter and is commonly taken to mean

    A. that is
    C. in the same place
    B. the same
    D. and others

Questions 22-37.

DIRECTIONS: Each of the sentences numbered 22 to 37 may be classified MOST appropriately under one of the following four categories:
- A. faulty because of incorrect grammar
- B. faulty because of incorrect punctuation
- C. faulty because of incorrect capitalization
- D. correct

Examine each sentence carefully. Then, in the correspondingly numbered space at the right, print the letter preceding the option which is the BEST of the four suggested above. All incorrect sentences contain but one type of error. Consider a sentence correct if it contains none of the types of errors mentioned, even though there may be other correct ways of expressing the same thought.

22. The desk, as well as the chairs, were moved out of the office. 22.___

23. The clerk whose production was greatest for the month won a day's vacation as first prize. 23.___

24. Upon entering the room, the employees were found hard at work at their desks. 24.___

25. John Smith our new employee always arrives at work on time. 25.___

26. Punish whoever is guilty of stealing the money. 26.___

27. Intelligent and persistent effort lead to success no matter what the job may be. 27.___

28. The secretary asked, "can you call again at three o'clock?" 28.___

29. He told us, that if the report was not accepted at the next meeting, it would have to be rewritten. 29.___

30. He would not have sent the letter if he had known that it would cause so much excitement. 30.___

31. We all looked forward to him coming to visit us. 31.___

32. If you find that you are unable to complete the assignment please notify me as soon as possible. 32.___

33. Every girl in the office went home on time but me; there was still some work for me to finish. 33.___

34. He wanted to know who the letter was addressed to, Mr. Brown or Mr. Smith. 34.___

35. "Mr. Jones, he said, please answer this letter as soon as possible." 35.___

36. The new clerk had an unusual accent inasmuch as he was born and educated in the south. 36.___

37. Although he is younger than her, he earns a higher salary. 37.___

Questions 38-45.

DIRECTIONS: Questions 38 to 45 consist of four words each. In each item, one of the words may be spelled incorrectly or all the words may be spelled correctly. If one of the words in an item is spelled incorrectly, print in the correspondingly numbered space at the right the letter preceding the word which is spelled incorrectly. If all four words are spelled correctly, print the letter E.

38.	A.	temporary	B.	existance	C.	complimentary	D.	altogether
39.	A.	privilege	B.	changeable	C.	jeopardize	D.	commitment
40.	A.	grievous	B.	alloted	C.	outrageous	D.	mortgage
41.	A.	tempermental	B.	bookkeeping				
	B.	accommodating	D.	panicky				
42.	A.	auxiliary	B.	indispensable	C.	ecstasy	D.	fiery
43.	A.	dissapear	B.	buoyant	C.	imminent	D.	parallel
44.	A.	loosly	B.	medicine	C.	schedule	D.	defendant
45.	A.	endeavor	B.	persuade	C.	retroactive	D.	desparate

Questions 46-50

DIRECTIONS: Each of Questions 46 to 50 contains five words in italics, one of which is not in keeping with the meaning which the question is evidently intended to carry. The five words in italics in each item are reprinted after the question. On the correspondingly numbered space at the right, print the letter preceding the one of the five words which does MOST to spoil the true meaning of the question.

46. City departments having direct *contact* with the *public* should be located *if* they are readily *accessible* to those *coming* to the office on business.

   A. contact   B. public   C. if
   D. accessible E. coming

47. Many communications covering a *specific* subject can be form letters, but going to *extremes* in this matter should be guarded against; to send a form letter when a specially *composed* letter should be used is *often* the most mistaken *extravagance*.

   A. specific   B. extremes   C. composed
   D. often   E. extravagance

48. In order to prevent *unavoidable* accidents, a *safety* engineer designs and superintends the *installation* of safety devices. If employees always used the safety devices *provided*, there would be *few* accidents.

   A. unavoidable B. safety   C. installation
   D. provided   E. few

49. Most business records have an intangible *value* to the business which *can* be measured in dollars and cents. They are the *result* of figures and facts obtained from many sources and are often *impossible* to replace at *any* cost of time or money. 49.____

   A. value   B. can   C. result   D. impossible   E. any

50. A major advantage gained by a company that uses only one *particular* type of a machine is greater *efficiency* of operation. If, for example, all the calculating machines in an office are identical, it is *trifling* that time is *saved* by employees in *learning* how to operate these machines. 50.____

   A. particular   B. efficiency   C. trifling
   D. saved   E. learning

KEY (CORRECT ANSWERS)

1. C	11. C	21. A	31. A	41. A
2. D	12. B	22. A	32. B	42. E
3. D	13. B	23. D	33. D	43. A
4. D	14. B	24. A	34. A	44. A
5. A	15. D	25. B	35. B	45. D
6. C	16. C	26. D	36. C	46. C
7. C	17. B	27. A	37. A	47. E
8. A	18. A	28. C	38. B	48. A
9. B	19. D	29. A	39. E	49. B
10. C	20. B	30. D	40. B	50. C

EXAMINATION SECTION
TEST 1

DIRECTIONS: Each question or incomplete statement is followed by several suggested answers or completions. Select the one that BEST answers the question or completes the statement. *PRINT THE LETTER OF THE CORRECT ANSWER IN THE SPACE AT THE RIGHT.*

Questions 1-10.

WORD MEANING

DIRECTIONS: Each question from 1 to 10 contains a word in capitals followed by four suggested meanings of the word. For each question, choose the best meaning. *PRINT THE LETTER OF THE CORRECT ANSWER IN THE SPACE AT THE RIGHT.*

1. ACCURATE
   A. correct   B. useful   C. afraid   D. careless

2. ALTER
   A. copy   B. change   C. report   D. agree

3. DOCUMENT
   A. outline   B. agreement   C. blueprint   D. record

4. INDICATE
   A. listen   B. show   C. guess   D. try

5. INVENTORY
   A. custom   B. discovery   C. warning   D. list

6. ISSUE
   A. annoy   B. use up   C. give out   D. gain

7. NOTIFY
   A. inform   B. promise   C. approve   D. strengthen

8. ROUTINE
   A. path   B. mistake   C. habit   D. journey

9. TERMINATE
   A. rest   B. start   C. deny   D. end

10. TRANSMIT
    A. put in   B. send   C. stop   D. go across

29

Questions 11-15.

READING COMPREHENSION

DIRECTIONS: Questions 11 through 15 test how well you understand what you read. It will be necessary for you to read carefully because your answers to these questions should be based ONLY on the information given in the following paragraphs.

The recipient gains an impression of a typewritten letter before he begins to read the message. Pastors which provide for a good first impression include margins and spacing that are visually pleasing, formal parts of the letter which are correctly placed according to the style of the letter, copy which is free of obvious erasures and over-strikes, and transcript that is even and clear. The problem for the typist is that of how to produce that first, positive impression of her work.

There are several general rules which a typist can follow when she wishes to prepare a properly spaced letter on a sheet of letter-head. Ordinarily, the width of a letter should not be less than four inches nor more than six inches. The side margins should also have a desirable relation to the bottom margin and the space between the letterhead and the body of the letter. Usually the most appealing arrangement is when the side margins are even and the bottom margin is slightly wider than the side margins. In some offices, however, standard line length is used for all business letters, and the secretary then varies the spacing between the date line and the inside address according to the length of the letter.

11. The BEST title for the above paragraphs would be: 11._____

    A. Writing Office Letters
    B. Making Good First Impressions
    C. Judging Well-Typed Letters
    D. Good Placing and Spacing for Office Letters

12. According to the above paragraphs, which of the following might be considered the way   12._____
    in which people very quickly judge the quality of work which has been typed? By

    A. measuring the margins to see if they are correct
    B. looking at the spacing and cleanliness of the typescript
    C. scanning the body of the letter for meaning
    D. reading the date line and address for errors

13. What, according to the above paragraphs, would be definitely UNDESIRABLE as the   13._____
    average line length of a typed letter?

    A. 4"   B. 5"   C. 6"   D. 7"

14. According to the above paragraphs, when the line length is kept standard, the secretary   14._____

    A. does not have to vary the spacing at all since this also is standard
    B. adjusts the spacing between the date line and inside address for different lengths of letters
    C. uses the longest line as a guideline for spacing between the date line and inside address
    D. varies the number of spaces between the lines

3 (#1)

15. According to the above paragraphs, side margins are MOST pleasing when they 15.____
    A. are even and somewhat smaller than the bottom margin
    B. are slightly wider than the bottom margin
    C. vary with the length of the letter
    D. are figured independently from the letterhead and the body of the letter

Questions 16-20.

CODING

DIRECTIONS:

Name of Applicant	H A N G S B R U K E
Test Code	c o m p l e x i t y
File Number	0 1 2 3 4 5 6 7 8 9

Assume that each of the above capital letters is the first letter of the name of an Applicant, that the small letter directly beneath each capital letter is the test code for the Applicant, and that the number directly beneath each code letter is the file number for the Applicant.

In each of the following Questions 16 through 20, the test code letters and the file numbers in Columns 2 and 3 should correspond to the capital letters in Column 1. For each question, look at each column carefully and mark your answer as follows:

    If there is an error only in Column 2, mark your answer A.
    If there is an error only in Column 3, mark your answer B.
    If there is an error in both Columns 2 and 3, mark your answer C.
    If both Columns 2 and 3 are correct, mark your answer D.

The following sample question is given to help you understand the procedure.

SAMPLE QUESTION

Column 1	Column 2	Column 3
AKEHN	otyci	18902

In Column 2, the final test code letter *i*. should be *m*. Column 3 is correctly coded to Column 1. Since there is an error only in Column 2, the answer is A.

	Column 1	Column 2	Column 3	
16.	NEKKU	mytti	29987	16.____
17.	KRAEB	txyle	86095	17.____
18.	ENAUK	ymoit	92178	18.____
19.	REANA	xeomo	69121	19.____
20.	EKHSE	ytcxy	97049	20.____

Questions 21-30.

ARITHMETICAL REASONING

21. If a secretary answered 28 phone calls and typed the addresses for 112 credit statements in one morning, what is the ratio of phone calls answered to credit statements typed for that period of time?

    A. 1:4   B. 1:7   C. 2:3   D. 3:5

22. According to a suggested filing system, no more than 10 folders should be filed behind any one file guide and from 15 to 25 file guides should be used in each file drawer for easy finding and filing.
    The maximum number of folders that a five-drawer file cabinet can hold to allow easy finding and filing is

    A. 550   B. 750   C. 1,100   D. 1,250

23. An employee had a starting salary of $25,804. He received a salary increase at the end of each year, and at the end of the seventh year his salary was $33,476.
    What was his average annual increase in salary over these seven years?

    A. $1,020   B. $1,076   C. $1,096   D. $1,144

24. The 55 typists and 28 senior clerks in a certain city agency were paid a total of $1,943,200 in salaries last year.
    If the average annual salary of a typist was $22,400 the average annual salary of a senior clerk was

    A. $25,400   B. $26,600   C. $26,800   D. $27,000

25. A typist has been given a three page report to type. She has finished typing the first two pages. The first page has 283 words, and the second page has 366 words.
    If the total report consists of 954 words, how many words will she have to type on the third page of the report?

    A. 202   B. 287   C. 305   D. 313

26. In one day, Clerk A processed 30% more forms than Clerk B, and Clerk C processed 1¼ times as many forms as Clerk A. If Clerk B processed 40 forms, how many more forms were processed by Clerk C than Clerk B?

    A. 12   B. 13   C. 21   D. 25

27. A clerk who earns a gross salary of $452 every two weeks has the following deductions taken from her paycheck:
    15% for City, State, Federal taxes; 2 1/2% for Social Security; $1.30 for health insurance; and $6.00 for union dues. The amount of her take-home pay is

    A. $256.20   B. $312.40   C. $331.60   D. $365.60

28. In 2005, a city agency spent $2,000 to buy pencils at a cost of $5.00 a dozen.
    If the agency used 3/4 of these pencils in 2005 and used the same number of pencils in 2006, how many more pencils did it have to buy to have enough pencils for all of 2006?

    A. 1,200   B. 2,400   C. 3,600   D. 4,800

29. A clerk who worked in Agency X earned the following salaries: $20,140 the first year, $21,000 the second year, and $21,920 the third year. Another clerk who worked in Agency Y for three years earned $21,100 a year for two years and $21,448 the third year. The difference between the average salaries received by both clerks over a three-year period is

   A. $196   B. $204   C. $348   D. $564

30. An employee who works over 40 hours in any week receives overtime payment for the extra hours at time and one-half (1 1/2 times) his hourly rate of pay. An employee who earns $13.60 an hour works a total of 45 hours during a certain week.
   His total pay for that week would be

   A. $564.40   B. $612.00   C. $646.00   D. $812.00

Questions 31-35.

RELATED INFORMATION

31. To tell a newly-employed clerk to fill a top drawer of a four-drawer cabinet with heavy folders which will be often used and to keep lower drawers only partly filled is

   A. *good*, because a tall person would have to bend unnecessarily if he had to use a lower drawer
   B. *bad*, because the file cabinet may tip over when the top drawer is opened
   C. *good*, because it is the most easily reachable drawer for the average person
   D. *bad*, because a person bending down at another drawer may accidentally bang his head on the bottom of the drawer when he straightens up

32. If a senior typist or senior clerk has requisitioned a *ream* of paper in order to duplicate a single page office announcement, how many announcements can be printed from the one package of paper?

   A. 200   B. 500   C. 700   D. 1,000

33. Your supervisor has asked you to locate a telephone number for an attorney named Jones, whose office is located at 311 Broadway, and whose name is not already listed in your files.
   The BEST method for finding the number would be for you to

   A. call the information operator and have her get it for you
   B. look in the alphabetical directory (white pages) under the name Jones at 311 Broadway
   C. refer to the heading Attorney in the yellow pages for the name Jones at 311 Broadway
   D. ask your supervisor who referred her to Mr. Jones, then call that person for the number

34. An example of material that should NOT be sent by first class mail is a

   A. email copy of a letter   B. post card
   C. business reply card   D. large catalogue

35. In the operations of a government agency, a voucher is ORDINARILY used to   35.____
    A. refer someone to the agency for a position or assignment
    B. certify that an agency's records of financial trans-actions are accurate
    C. order payment from agency funds of a stated amount to an individual
    D. enter a statement of official opinion in the records of the agency

Questions 36-40.

ENGLISH USAGE

DIRECTIONS: Each question from 36 through 40 contains a sentence. Read each sentence carefully to decide whether it is correct. Then, in the space at the right, mark your answer:

(A) if the sentence is incorrect because of bad grammar or sentence structure

(B) if the sentence is incorrect because of bad punctuation

(C) if the sentence is incorrect because of bad capitalization

(D) if the sentence is correct

Each incorrect sentence has only one type of error. Consider a sentence correct if it has no errors, although there may be other correct ways of saying the same thing.

SAMPLE QUESTION I: One of our clerks were promoted yesterday.

The subject of this sentence is *one,* so the verb should be *was promoted* instead of *were promoted.* Since the sentence is incorrect because of bad grammar, the answer to Sample Question I is (A).

SAMPLE QUESTION II: Between you and me, I would prefer not going there.

Since this sentence is correct, the answer to Sample Question II is (D).

36. The National alliance of Businessmen is trying to persuade private businesses to hire youth in the summertime.   36.____

37. The supervisor who is on vacation, is in charge of processing vouchers.   37.____

38. The activity of the committee at its conferences is always stimulating.   38.____

39. After checking the addresses again, the letters went to the mailroom.   39.____

40. The director, as well as the employees, are interested in sharing the dividends.   40.____

Questions 41-45.

FILING

DIRECTIONS: Each question from 41 through 45 contains four names. For each question, choose the name that should be FIRST if the four names are to be arranged in alphabeti-cal order in accordance with the Rules for Alphabetical Filing given below. Read these rules carefully. Then, for each question, indicate in the space at the right the letter before the name that should be FIRST in alphabetical order.

RULES FOR ALPHABETICAL FILING

Names of People

(1) The names of people are filed in strict alphabetical order, first according to the last name, then according to first name or initial, and finally according to middle name or initial. FOR EXAMPLE: George Allen comes before Edward Bell, and Leonard P. Reston comes before Lucille B. Reston.

(2) When last names are the same, FOR EXAMPLE, A. Green and Agnes Green, the one with the initial comes before the one with the name written out when the first initials are identical.

(3) When first and last names are alike and the middle name is given, FOR EXAMPLE, John David Doe and John Devoe Doe, the names should be filed in the alphabetical order of the middle names.

(4) When first and last names are the same, a name without a middle initial comes before one with a middle name or initial. FOR EXAMPLE, John Doe comes before both John A. Doe and John Alan Doe.

(5) When first and last names are the same, a name with a middle initial comes before one with a middle name beginning with the same initial. FOR EXAMPLE: Jack R. Hertz comes before Jack Richard Hertz.

(6) Prefixes such as De, O', Mac, Mc, and Van are filed as written and are treated as part of the names to which they are connected. FOR EXAMPLE: Robert O'Dea is filed before David Olsen.

(7) Abbreviated names are treated as if they were spelled out. FOR EXAMPLE: Chas. is filed as Charles and Thos. is filed as Thomas.

(8) Titles and designations such as Dr., Mr., and Prof, are disregarded in filing.

Names of Organizations

(1) The names of business organizations are filed according to the order in which each word in the name appears. When an organization name bears the name of a person, it is filed according to the rules for filing names of people as given above. FOR EXAMPLE: William Smith Service Co. comes before Television Distributors, Inc.

(2) Where bureau, board, office, or department appears as the first part of the title of a governmental agency, that agency should be filed under the word in the title expressing the chief function of the agency. FOR EXAMPLE: Bureau of the Budget would be filed as if written Budget, (Bureau of the). The Department of Personnel would be filed as if written Personnel, (Department of).

(3) When the following words are part of an organization, they are disregarded: the, of, and.

(4) When there are numbers in a name, they are treated as if they were spelled out. FOR EXAMPLE: 10th Street Bootery is filed as Tenth Street Bootery.

SAMPLE QUESTION:
- A. Jane Earl (2)
- B. James A. Earle (4)
- C. James Earl (1)
- D. J. Earle (3)

The numbers in parentheses show the proper alphabetical order in which these names should be filed. Since the name that should be filed FIRST is James Earl, the answer to the Sample Question is (C).

41.
- A. Majorca Leather Goods
- B. Robert Maiorca and Sons
- C. Maintenance Management Corp.
- D. Majestic Carpet Mills

42.
- A. Municipal Telephone Service
- B. Municipal Reference Library
- C. Municipal Credit Union
- D. Municipal Broadcasting System

43.
- A. Robert B. Pierce
- B. R. Bruce Pierce
- C. Ronald Pierce
- D. Robert Bruce Pierce

44.
- A. Four Seasons Sports Club
- B. 14th. St. Shopping Center
- C. Forty Thieves Restaurant
- D. 42nd St. Theaters

45.
- A. Franco Franceschini
- B. Amos Franchini
- C. Sandra Franceschia
- D. Lilie Franchinesca

Questions 46-50.

SPELLING

DIRECTIONS: In each question, one of the words is misspelled. Select the letter of the misspelled word. *PRINT THE LETTER OF THE CORRECT ANSWER IN THE SPACE AT THE RIGHT.*

46.
- A. option
- B. extradite
- C. comparitive
- D. jealousy

47.
- A. handicaped
- B. assurance
- C. sympathy
- D. speech

48. A. recommend   B. carraige
    C. disapprove D. independent   48._____

49. A. ingenuity   B. tenet (opinion)
    C. uncanny   D. intrigueing   49._____

50. A. arduous   B. hideous
    C. iervant   D. companies   50._____

KEY (CORRECT ANSWERS)

1. A	11. D	21. A	31. B	41. C
2. B	12. B	22. D	32. B	42. D
3. D	13. D	23. C	33. C	43. B
4. B	14. B	24. A	34. D	44. D
5. D	15. A	25. C	35. C	45. C
6. C	16. B	26. D	36. C	46. C
7. A	17. C	27. D	37. B	47. A
8. C	18. D	28. B	38. D	48. B
9. D	19. A	29. A	39. A	49. D
10. B	20. C	30. C	40. A	50. C'

EXAMINATION SECTION
TEST 1

DIRECTIONS: Each question or incomplete statement is followed by several suggested answers or completions. Select the one that BEST answers the question or completes the statement. *PRINT THE LETTER OF THE CORRECT ANSWER IN THE SPACE AT THE RIGHT.*

Questions 1-5.

DIRECTIONS: Questions 1 through 5 consist of a sentence with an underlined word. For each question, select the choice that is CLOSEST in meaning to the underlined word.

   EXAMPLE
   This division reviews the fiscal reports of the agency.
   In this sentence, the word *fiscal* means MOST NEARLY
         A. financial   B. critical   C. basic   D. personnel
   The correct answer is A. "financial" because "financial" is closest to *fiscal*.
   Therefore, the answer is A.

1. Every good office worker needs basic skills.
   The word *basic* in this sentence means
      A. fundamental   B. advanced   C. unusual   D. outstanding

2. He turned out to be a good instructor.
   The word *instructor* in this sentence means
      A. student   B. worker   C. typist   D. teacher

3. The quantity of work in the office was under study.
   In this sentence, the word *quantity* means
      A. amount   B. flow   C. supervision   D. type

4. The morning was spent examining the time records.
   In this sentence, the word *examining* means
      A. distributing   B. collecting   C. checking   D. filing

5. The candidate filled in the proper spaces on the form.
   In this sentence, the word *proper* means
      A. blank   B. appropriate   C. many   D. remaining

Questions 6-8.

DIRECTIONS: Questions 6 through 8 are to be answered SOLELY on the basis of the information contained in the following paragraph.

The increase in the number of public documents in the last two centuries closely matches the increase in population in the United States. The great number of public documents has become a serious threat to their usefulness. It is necessary to have programs which will reduce the number of public documents that are kept and which will, at the same time, assure keeping those that have value. Such programs need a great deal of thought to have any success.

6. According to the above paragraph, public documents may be less useful if
   A. the files are open to the public
   B. the record room is too small
   C. the copying machine is operated only during normal working hours
   D. too many records are being kept

6._____

7. According to the above paragraph, the growth of the population in the United States has matched the growth in the quantity of public documents for a period of MOST NEARLY _____ years.
   A. 50   B. 100   C. 200   D. 300

7._____

8. According to the above paragraph, the increased number of public documents has made it necessary to
   A. find out which public documents are worth keeping
   B. reduce the great number of public documents by decreasing government services
   C. eliminate the copying of all original public documents
   D. avoid all new copying devices

8._____

Questions 9-10.

DIRECTIONS: Questions 9 and 10 are to be answered SOLELY on the basis of the information contained in the following paragraph.

The work goals of an agency can best be reached if the employees understand and agree with these goals. One way to gain such understanding and agreement is for management to encourage and seriously consider suggestions from employees in the setting of agency goals.

9. On the basis of the above paragraph, the BEST way to achieve the work goals of an agency is to
   A. make certain that employees work as hard as possible
   B. study the organizational structure of the agency
   C. encourage employees to think seriously about the agency's problems
   D. stimulate employee understanding of the work goals

9._____

10. On the basis of the above paragraph, understanding and agreement with agency goals can be gained by
    A. allowing the employees to set agency goals
    B. reaching agency goals quickly
    C. legislative review of agency operations
    D. employee participation in setting agency goals

10.____

Questions 11-15.

DIRECTIONS: Each of Questions 11 through 15 consists of a group of four words. One word in each group is incorrectly spelled. For each question, print the letter of the correct answer in the space at the right that is the same as the letter next to the word which is INCORRECTLY spelled.

EXAMPLE

A. housing   B. certain   C. budgit   D. money

The word "budgit" is incorrectly spelled, because the correct spelling should be "budget." Therefore, the correct answer is C.

11. A. sentince   B. bulletin   C. notice   D. definition   11.____
12. A. appointment B. exactly   C. typest   D. light   12.____
13. A. penalty   B. suparvise   C. consider   D. division   13.____
14. A. schedule   B. accurate   C. corect   D. simple   14.____
15. A. suggestion   B. installed   C. proper   D. agincy   15.____

Questions 16-20.

DIRECTIONS: Each Question 16 through 20 consists of a sentence which may be
    A. incorrect because of bad word usage, or
    B. incorrect because of bad punctuation, or
    C. incorrect because of bad spelling, or
    D. correct
Read each sentence carefully. Then print in the space at the right A, B, C, or D, according to the answer you choose from the four choices listed above. There is only one type of error in each incorrect sentence. If there is no error, the sentence is correct.

EXAMPLE

George Washington was the father of his contry.
This sentence is incorrect because of bad spelling ("contry" instead of "country").
Therefore, the answer is C.

16. The assignment was completed in record time but the payroll for it has not yet been preparid. 16._____

17. The operator, on the other hand, is willing to learn me how to use the mimeograph. 17._____

18. She is the prettiest of the three sisters. 18._____

19. She doesn't know; if the mail has arrived. 19._____

20. The doorknob of the office door is broke. 20._____

21. A clerk can process a form in 15 minutes.
    How many forms can that clerk process in six hours?
    A. 10   B. 21   C. 24   D. 90   21._____

22. An office staff consists of 120 people. Sixty of them have been assigned to a special project. Of the remaining staff, 20 answer the mail, 10 handle phone calls, and the rest operate the office machines.
    The number of people operating the office machines is
    A. 20   B. 30   C. 40   D. 45   22._____

23. An office worker received 65 applications but on the first day had to return 26 of them for being incomplete and on the second day 25 had to be returned for being incomplete.
    How many applications did NOT have to be returned?
    A. 10   B. 12   C. 14   D. 16   23._____

24. An office worker answered 63 phone calls in one day and 91 phone calls the next day.
    For these 2 days, what was the average number of phone calls he answered per day?
    A. 77   B. 28   C. 82   D. 93   24._____

25. An office worker processed 12 vouchers of $8.50 each, 3 vouchers of $3.68 each, and 2 vouchers of $1.29 each.
    The TOTAL dollar amount of these vouchers is
    A. $116.04   B. $117.52   C. $118.62   D. $119.04   25._____

KEY (CORRECT ANSWERS)

1.	A	11.	A
2.	D	12.	C
3.	A	13.	B
4.	C	14.	C
5.	B	15.	D
6.	D	16.	C
7.	C	17.	A
8.	A	18.	D
9.	D	19.	B
10.	D	20.	A

21. C
22. B
23. C
24. A
25. C

TEST 2

DIRECTIONS: Each question or incomplete statement is followed by several suggested answers or completions. Select the one that BEST answers the question or completes the statement. *PRINT THE LETTER OF THE CORRECT ANSWER IN THE SPACE AT THE RIGHT.*

Questions 1-5.

DIRECTIONS: Each Question from 1 through 5 lists four names. The names may not be exactly the same. Compare the names in each question and mark your answer
    A if all the names are different
    B if only two names are exactly the same
    C if only three names are exactly the same
    D if all four names are exactly the same
                    EXAMPLE
                Jensen, Alfred E.
                Jensen, Alfred E.
                Jensan, Alfred E.
                Jensen, Fred E.

Since the name Jensen, Alfred E. appears twice and is exactly the same in both places, the correct answer is B.

1. A. Riviera, Pedro S.   B. Rivers, Pedro S.   1._____
   C. Riviera, Pedro N.   D. Riviera, Juan S.

2. A. Guider, Albert   B. Guidar, Albert   2._____
   C. Giuder, Alfred   D. Guider, Albert

3. A. Blum, Rona   B. Blum, Rona   3._____
   C. Blum, Rona   D. Blum, Rona

4. A. Raugh, John   B. Raugh, James   4._____
   C. Raughe, John   D. Raugh, John

5. A. Katz, Stanley   B. Katz, Stanley   5._____
   C. Katze, Stanley   D. Katz, Stanley

Questions 6-10.

DIRECTIONS: Each Question 6 through 10 consists of numbers or letters in Columns I and II. For each question, compare each line of Column I with its corresponding line in Column II and decide how many lines in Column I are EXACTLY the same as their corresponding lines in Column II. In your answer space, mark your answer
    A if only ONE line in Column I is exactly the same as its corresponding line in Column II
    B if only TWO lines in Column I are exactly the same as their corresponding lines in Column II

2 (#2)

  C if only THREE lines in Column I are exactly the same as their corresponding lines in Column II
  D if all FOUR lines in Column I are exactly the same as their corresponding lines in Column II

EXAMPLE

Column I	Column II
1776	1776
1865	1865
1945	1945
1976	1978

Only three lines in Column I are exactly the same as their corresponding lines in Column II. Therefore, the correct answer is C.

	Column I	Column II	
6.	5653	5653	6._____
	8727	8728	
	ZPSS	ZPSS	
	4952	9453	
7.	PNJP	PNPJ	7._____
	NJPJ	NJPJ	
	JNPN	JNPN	
	PNJP	PNPJ	
8.	effe	eFfe	8._____
	uWvw	uWvw	
	KpGj	KpGg	
	vmnv	vmnv	
9.	5232	5232	9._____
	PfrC	PfrN	
	zssz	zzss	
	rwwr	rwww	
10.	czws	czws	10._____
	cecc	cece	
	thrm	thrm	
	lwtz	lwtz	

Questions 11-15.

DIRECTIONS: Questions 11 through 15 have lines of letters and numbers. Each letter should be matched with its number in accordance with the following table.

Letter	F	R	C	A	W	L	E	N	B	T
Matching Number	0	1	2	3	4	5	6	7	8	9

45

From the table you can determine that the letter F has the matching number 0 below it, the letter R has the matching number 1 below, etc.

For each question, compare each line of letters and numbers carefully to see if each letter has its correct matching number. If all the letters and numbers are matched correctly in

none of the lines of the question, mark your answer A
only *one* of the lines of the question, mark your answer B
only *two* of the lines of the question, mark your answer C
all three lines of the question, mark your answer D

EXAMPLE
WBCR   4826
TLBF   9580
ATNE   3986

There is a mistake in the first line because the letter R should have its matching number 1 instead of the number 6.

The second line is correct because each letter shown has the correct matching number.

There is a mistake in the third line because the letter N should have the matching number 7 instead of the number 8.

Since all the letters and numbers are correct matched in only one of the lines in the sample, the correct answer is B.

11. EBCT   6829
    ATWR   3961
    NLBW   7584

12. RNCT   1729
    LNCR   5728
    WAEB   5368

13. NTWB   7948
    RABL   1385
    TAEF   9360

14. LWRB   5417
    RLWN   1647
    CBWA   2843

15. ABTC   3792
    WCER   5261
    AWCN   3417

16. Your job often brings you into contact with the public.
    Of the following, it would be MOST desirable to explain the reasons for official actions to people coming into your office for assistance because such explanations
    A. help build greater understanding between the public and your agency
    B. help build greater self-confidence in city employees
    C. convince the public that nothing they do can upset a city employee
    D. show the public that city employees are intelligent

17. Assume that you strongly dislike one of your co-workers.
 You should FIRST
 A. discuss your feeling with the co-worker
 B. demand a transfer to another office
 C. suggest to your supervisor that the co-worker should be observed carefully
 D. try to figure out the reason for this dislike before you say or do anything

18. An office worker who has problems accepting authority is MOST likely to find it difficult to
 A. obey rules
 B. understand people
 C. assist other employees
 D. follow complex instructions

19. The employees in your office have taken a dislike to one person and frequently annoy her.
 Your supervisor should
 A. transfer this person to another unit at the first opportunity
 B. try to find out the reason for the staff's attitude before doing anything about it
 C. threaten to transfer the first person observed bothering this person
 D. ignore the situation

20. Assume that your supervisor has asked a worker in your office to get a copy of a report out of the files. You notice the worker as accidentally pulled out the wrong report.
 Of the following, the BEST way for you to handle this situation is to tell
 A. the worker about all the difficulties that will result from this error
 B. the worker about her mistake in a nice way
 C. the worker to ignore this error
 D. your supervisor that this worker needs more training in how to use the files

21. Filing systems differ in their efficiency.
 Which of the following is the BEST way to evaluate the efficiency of a filing system? A
 A. number of times used per day
 B. amount of material that is received each day for filing
 C. amount of time it takes to locate material
 D. type of locking system used

22. In planning ahead so that a sufficient amount of general office supplies is always available, it would be LEAST important to find out the
 A. current office supply needs of the staff
 B. amount of office supplies used last year
 C. days and times that office supplies can be ordered
 D. agency goals and objectives

23. The MAIN reason for establishing routine office work procedures is that once a routine is established
    A. work need not be checked for accuracy
    B. all steps in the routine will take an equal amount of time to perform
    C. each time the job is repeated, it will take less time to perform
    D. each step in the routine will not have to be planned all over again each time

23._____

24. When an office machine centrally located in an agency must be shut down for repairs, the bureaus and divisions using this machine should be informed of the
    A. expected length of time before the machine will be in operation again
    B. estimated cost of repairs
    C. efforts being made to avoid future repairs
    D. type of new equipment which the agency may buy in the future to replace the machine being repaired

24._____

25. If the day's work is properly scheduled, the MOST important result would be that the
    A. supervisor will not have to do much supervision
    B. employee will know what to do next
    C. employee will show greater initiative
    D. job will become routine

25._____

KEY (CORRECT ANSWERS)

1.	A		11.	C
2.	B		12.	B
3.	D		13.	D
4.	B		14.	B
5.	C		15.	A
6.	B		16.	A
7.	B		17.	D
8.	B		18.	A
9.	A		19.	B
10.	C		20.	B

21.	C
22.	D
23.	D
24.	A
25.	B

EXAMINATION SECTION
TEST 1

DIRECTIONS: Each question or incomplete statement is followed by several suggested answers or completions. Select the one that BEST answers the question or completes the statement. *PRINT THE LETTER OF THE CORRECT ANSWER IN THE SPACE AT THE RIGHT.*

1. Assume that a few co-workers meet near your desk and talk about personal matters during working hours. Lately, this practice has interfered with your work.
In order to stop this practice, the BEST action for you to take FIRST is to
   A. ask your supervisor to put a stop to the co-workers' meeting near your desk
   B. discontinue any friendship with this group
   C. ask your co-workers not to meet near your desk
   D. request that your desk be moved to another location

   1._____

2. In order to maintain office coverage during working hours, your supervisor has scheduled your lunch hour from 1 P.M. to 2 P.M. and your co-workers' lunch hour from 12 P.M. to 1 P.M. Lately, your co-worker has been returning late from lunch each day. As a result, you don't get a full hour since you must return to the office by 2 P.M.
Of the following, the BEST action for you to take FIRST is to
   A. explain to your co-worker in a courteous manner that his lateness is interfering with your right to a full hour for lunch
   B. tell your co-worker that his lateness must stop or you will report him to your supervisor
   C. report your co-worker's lateness to your supervisor
   D. leave at 1 P.M. for lunch, whether your co-worker has returned or not

   2._____

3. Assume that, as an office worker, one of your jobs is to open mail sent to your unit, read the mail for content, and send the mail to the appropriate person to handle. You accidentally open and begin to read a letter marked *personal* to a co-worker.
Of the following, the BEST action for you to take is to
   A. report to your supervisor that your co-worker is receiving personal mail at the office
   B. destroy the letter so that your co-worker does not know you saw it
   C. reseal the letter and place it on the co-worker's desk without saying anything
   D. bring the letter to your co-worker and explain that you opened it by accident

   3._____

4. Suppose that in evaluating your work, your supervisor gives you an overall rating, but states that you sometimes turn in work with careless errors.
The BEST action for you to take would be to
   A. ask a co-worker who is good at details to proofread your work
   B. take time to do a careful job, paying more attention to detail
   C. continue working as usual since occasional errors are to be expected
   D. ask your supervisor if she would mind correcting your errors

4.____

5. Assume that you are taking a telephone message for a co-worker who is not in the office at the time.
Of the following, the LEAST important item to write on the message is the
   A. length of the call   B. name of the caller
   C. time of the call   D. telephone number of the caller

5.____

Questions 6-13.

DIRECTIONS: Questions 6 through 13 each consist of a sentence which may or may not be an example of good English. The underlined parts of each sentence may be correct or incorrect. Examine each sentence, considering grammar, punctuation, spelling, and capitalization. If the English usage in the underlined parts of the sentence given is better than any of the changes in the underlined words suggested in Options B, C, or D, choose Option A. If the changes in the underlined words suggested in Options B, C, or D would make the sentence correct, choose the correct option. Do not choose an option that will change the meaning of the sentence.

6. This Fall, the office will be closed on Columbus Day, October 9th.
   A. Correct as is   B. fall...Columbus Day, October
   C. Fall...Columbus day, October   D. fall...Columbus Day, october

6.____

7. This manual discribes the duties performed by an Office Aide.
   A. Correct as is   B. describe the duties performed
   C. discribe the duties performed   D. describes the duties performed

7.____

8. There weren't no paper in the supply closet.
   A. Correct as is   B. weren't any
   C. wasn't any   D. wasn't no

8.____

9. The new employees left there office to attend a meeting.
   A. Correct as is   B. they're
   C. their   D. thier

9.____

10. The office worker started working at 8:30 a.m.
    A. Correct as is   B. 8:30 a.m.
    C. 8;30 a,m.   D. 8:30 am.

10.____

11. The alphabet, or A to Z sequence are the basis of most filing systems.
    A. Correct as is   B. alphabet, or A to Z sequence, is
    C. alphabet, or A to Z sequence are   D. alphabet, or A too Z sequence, is

11.____

12. Those file cabinets are five feet tall. 12.____
    A. Correct as is   B. Them…feet
    C. Those…foot   D. Them…foot

13. The Office Aide checked the register and finding the date of the meeting. 13.____
    A. Correct as is   B. regaster and finding
    C. register and found   D. regaster and found

Questions 14-21.

DIRECTIONS: Each of Questions 14 through 21 has two lists of numbers. Each list contains three sets of numbers. Check each of the three sets in the list on the right to see if they are the same as the corresponding set in the list on the left. Mark your answers
   A. if none of the sets in the right list are the same as those in the left list
   B. if only one of the sets in the right list are the same as those in the left list
   C. if only two of the sets in the right list are the same as those in the left list
   D. if all three sets in the right list are the same as those in the left list

14. 7354183476   7354983476   14.____
     4474747744   4474747774
     57914302311   57914302311

15. 7143592185   7143892185   15.____
     8344517699   8344518699
     9178531263   9178531263

16. 2572114731   257214731   16.____
     8806835476   8806835476
     8255831246   8255831246

17. 331476853821   331476858621   17.____
     6976658532996   6976655832996
     3766042113715   3766042113745

18. 8806663315   8806663315   18.____
     74477138449   74477138449
     211756663666   211756663666

19. 990006966996   99000696996   19.____
     53022219743   53022219843
     4171171117717   4171171177717

20. 24400222433004   24400222433004   20.____
     5300030055000355   5300030055500355
     20000075532002022   20000075532002022

4 (#1)

21. 6111666406600001116   61116664066001116   21._____
    7111300117001100733   7111300117001100733
    26666446664476518   26666446664476518

Questions 22-25.

DIRECTIONS: Each of Questions 22 through 25 has two lists of names and addresses. Each list contains three sets of names and addresses. Check each of the three sets in the list on the right to see if they are the same as the corresponding set in the list on the left. Mark your answers
    A. if none of the sets in the right list are the same as those in the left list
    B. if only one of the sets in the right list are the same as those in the left list
    C. if only two of the sets in the right list are the same as those in the left list
    D. if all three sets in the right list are the same as those in the left list

22.   Mary T. Berlinger   Mary T. Berlinger   22._____
       2351 Hampton St.   2351 Hampton St.
       Monsey, N.Y. 20117   Monsey, N.Y. 20117

       Eduardo Benes   Eduardo Benes
       473 Kingston Avenue   473 Kingston Avenue
       Central Islip, N.Y. 11734   Central Islip, N.Y. 11734

       Alan Carrington Fuchs   Alan Carrington Fuchs
       17 Gnarled Hollow Road   17 Gnarled Hollow Road
       Los Angeles, CA 91635   Los Angeles, CA 91685

23.   David John Jacobson   David John Jacobson   23._____
       178 35 St. Apt. 4C   178 53 St. Apt. 4C
       New York, N.Y. 00927   New York, N.Y. 00927

       Ann-Marie Calonella   Ann-Marie Calonella
       7243 South Ridge Blvd.   7243 South Ridge Blvd.
       Bakersfield, CA 96714   Bakersfield, CA 96714

       Pauline M. Thompson   Pauline M. Thomson
       872 Linden Ave.   872 Linden Ave.
       Houston, Texas 70321   Houston, Texas 70321

24.   Chester LeRoy Masterton   Chester LeRoy Masterson   24._____
       152 Lacy Rd.   152 Lacy Rd.
       Kankakee, Ill. 54532   Kankakee, Ill. 54532

       William Maloney   William Maloney
       S. LaCrosse Pla.   S. LaCross Pla.
       Wausau, Wisconsin 52146   Wausau, Wisconsin 52146

5 (#1)

    Cynthia V. Barnes
    16 Pines Rd.
    Greenpoint, Miss. 20376

25. Marcel Jean Frontenac
    6 Burton On The Water
    Calender, Me. 01471

    J. Scott Marsden
    174 S. Tipton St.
    Cleveland, Ohio

    Lawrence T. Haney
    171 McDonough St.
    Decatur, Ga. 31304

Cynthia V. Barnes
16 Pines Rd.
Greenpoint, Miss. 20376

Marcel Jean Frontenac   25.____
6 Burton On The Water
Calender, Me. 01471

J. Scott Marsden
174 Tipton St.
Cleveland, Ohio

Lawrence T. Haney
171 McDonough St.
Decatur, Ga. 31304

KEY (CORRECT ANSWERS)

1.	C		11.	B
2.	A		12.	A
3.	D		13.	C
4.	B		14.	B
5.	A		15.	B
6.	B		16.	C
7.	D		17.	A
8.	C		18.	D
9.	C		19.	A
10.	B		20.	C

21. C
22. C
23. B
24. B
25. C

TEST 2

DIRECTIONS: Each question or incomplete statement is followed by several suggested answers or completions. Select the one that BEST answers the question or completes the statement. *PRINT THE LETTER OF THE CORRECT ANSWER IN THE SPACE AT THE RIGHT.*

Questions 1-6.

DIRECTIONS: Questions 1 through 6 are to be answered SOLELY on the basis of the information contained in the following passage.

Duplicating is the process of making a number of identical copies of letters, document, etc. from an original. Some duplicating processes make copies directly from the original document. Other duplicating processes require the preparation of a special master, and copies are then made from the master. Four of the most common duplicating processes are stencil, fluid, offset, and xerox.

In the stencil process, the typewriter is used to cut the words into a master called a stencil. Drawings, charts, or graphs can be cut into the stencil using a stylus. As many as 3,500 good-quality copies can be reproduced from one stencil. Various grades of finished paper from inexpensive mimeograph to expensive bond can be used.

The fluid process is a good method of copying from 50 to 125 good-quality copies from a master, which is prepared with a special dye. The master is placed on the duplicator, and special paper with a hard finish is moistened and then passed through the duplicator. Some of the dye on the master is dissolved, creating an impression on the paper. The impression becomes lighter as more copies are made; and once the dye on the master is used up, a new master must be made.

The offset process is the most adaptable office duplicating process because this process can be used for making a few copies or many copies. Masters can be made on paper or plastic for a few hundred copies, or on metal plates for as many as 75,000 copies. By using a special technique called photo-offset, charts, photographs, illustrations, or graphs can be reproduced on the master plate. The offset process is capable of producing large quantities of fine, top-quality copies on all types of finished paper.

The xerox process reproduces an exact duplicate from an original. It is the fastest duplicating method because the original material is placed directly on the duplicator, eliminating the need to make a special master. Any kind of paper can be used. The xerox process is the most expensive duplicating process; however, it is the best method of reproducing small quantities of good-quality copies of reports, letters, official documents, memos, or contracts.

1. Of the following, the MOST efficient method of reproducing 5,000 copies of a graph is
   A. stencil   B. fluid   C. offset   D. xerox

1.____

2. The offset process is the MOST adaptable office duplicating process because
   A. it is the quickest duplicating method
   B. it is the least expensive duplicating method
   C. it can produce a small number or large number of copies
   D. a softer master can be used over and over again

3. Which one of the following duplicating processes uses moistened paper?
   A. Stencil   B. Fluid   C. Offset   D. Xerox

4. The fluid process would be the BEST process to use for reproducing
   A. five copies of a school transcript
   B. fifty copies of a memo
   C. five hundred copies of a form letter
   D. five thousand copies of a chart

5. Which one of the following duplicating processes does NOT require a special master?
   A. Fluid   B. Xerox   C. Offset   D. Stencil

6. Xerox is NOT used for all duplicating jobs because
   A. it produces poor-quality copies
   B. the process is too expensive
   C. preparing the master is too time-consuming
   D. it cannot produce written reports

7. Assume a city agency has 775 office workers.
   If 2 out of 25 office workers were absent on a particular day, how many office workers reported to work on that day?
   A. 713   B. 744   C. 750   D. 773

Questions 8-11,

DIRECTIONS: In Questions 8 through 11, select the choice that is CLOSEST in meaning to the underlined word.

SAMPLE: This division reviews the fiscal reports of the agency.
In this sentence, the word *fiscal* means MOST NEARLY
A. financial   B. critical   C. basic   D. personnel

The correct answer is A, financial, because financial is closest to *fiscal*.

8. A central file eliminates the need to retain duplicate material.
The word *retain* means MOST NEARLY
A. keep   B. change   C. locate   D. process

9. Filing is a routine office task.
Routine means MOST NEARLY
A. proper   B. regular   C. simple   D. difficult

10. Sometimes a word, phrase, or sentence must be underlined to correct an error. 10.____
    Deleted means MOST NEARLY
    A. removed   B. added   C. expanded   D. improved

11. Your supervisor will evaluate your work. 11.____
    Evaluate means MOST NEARLY
    A. judge   B. list   C. assign   D. explain

Questions 12-19.

DIRECTIONS: The code table below shows 10 letters with matching numbers. For each Question 12 through 19, there are three sets of letters. Each set of letters is followed by a set of numbers which may or may not match their correct letter according to the code table. For each question, check all three sets of letters and numbers and mark your answer
  A. if no pairs are correctly matched
  B. if only one pair is correctly matched
  C. if only two pairs are correctly matched
  D. if all three pairs are correctly matched

CODE TABLE

T	M	V	D	S	P	R	G	B	H
1	2	3	4	5	6	7	8	9	0

SAMPLE QUESTION: TMVDSP   123456
                   RGBHTM   789011
                   DSPRGB   256789

In the sample question above, the first set of numbers correctly matches its set of letters. But the second and third pairs contain mistakes. In the second pair, M is incorrectly matched with number 1. According to the code table, letter M should be correctly matched with number 2. In the third pair, the letter D is incorrectly matched with number 2. According to the code table, letter D should be correctly matched with number 4. Since only one of the pairs is correctly matched, the answer to this sample question is B.

12. RSBMRM   759262   12.____
    GDSRVH   845730
    VDBRTM   349713

13. TGVSDR   183247   13.____
    SMHRDP   520647
    TRMHSR   172057

14. DSPRGM   456782   14.____
    MVDBHT   234902
    HPMDBT   062491

15. BVPTRD   936184   15.____
     GDPHMB   807029
     GMRHMV   827032

16. MGVRSH   283750   16.____
     TRDMBS   174295
     SPRMGV   567283

17. SGBSDM   489542   17.____
     MGHPTM   290612
     MPBMHT   269301

18. TDPBHM   146902   18.____
     VPBMRS   369275
     GDMBHM   842902

19. MVPTBV   236194   19.____
     PDRTMB   647128
     BGTMSM   981232

Questions 20-25.

DIRECTIONS: In each of Questions 20 through 25, the names of four people are given. For each question, choose as your answer the one of the four names given which should be filed FIRST according to the usual system of alphabetical filing of names, as described in the following paragraph.

In filing names, you must start with the last name. Names are filed in order of the first letter of the last name, then the second letter, etc. Therefore, BAILY would be filed before BROWN, which would be filed before COLT. A name with fewer letters of the same type comes first; i.e., Smith before Smithe. If the last names are the same, the names are filed alphabetically by the first name. If the first name is an initial, a name with an initial would come before a first name that starts with the same letter as the initial. Therefore, I. BROWN would come before IRA BROWN. Finally, if both last name and first name are the same, the name would be filed alphabetically by the middle name, one again an initial coming before a middle name which starts with the same letter as the initial. If there is no middle name at all, the name would come before those with middle initials or names.

SAMPLE QUESTION: A. Lester Daniels
                   B. William Dancer
                   C. Nathan Danzig
                   D. Dan Lester

The last names beginning with D are filed before the last name beginning with L. Since DANIELS, DANCER, and DANZIG all begin with the same three letters, you must look at the fourth letter of the last name to determine which name should be filed first. C comes before I or Z in the alphabet, so DANCER is filed before DANIELS or DANZIG. Therefore, the answer to the above sample question is B.

20. A. Scott Biala B. Mary Byala 20.____
    C. Martin Baylor D. Francis Bauer

21. A. Howard J. Black B. Howard Black 21.____
    C. J. Howard Black D. John H. Black

22. A. Theodora Garth Kingston B. Theadore Barth Kingston 22.____
    C. Thomas Kingston D. Thomas T. Kingston

23. A. Paulette Mary Huerta B. Paul M. Huerta 23.____
    C. Paulette L. Huerta D. Peter A. Huerta

24. A. Martha Hunt Morgan B. Martin Hunt Morgan 24.____
    C. Mary H. Morgan D. Martine H. Morgan

25. A. James T. Meerschaum B. James M. Mershum 25.____
    C. James F. Mearshaum D. James N. Meshum

KEY (CORRECT ANSWERS)

1.	C	11.	A
2.	C	12.	B
3.	B	13.	B
4.	B	14.	C
5.	B	15.	A
6.	B	16.	D
7.	A	17.	A
8.	A	18.	D
9.	B	19.	A
10.	A	20.	D

21. B
22. B
23. B
24. A
25. C

TEST 3

DIRECTIONS: Each question or incomplete statement is followed by several suggested answers or completions. Select the one that BEST answers the question or completes the statement. *PRINT THE LETTER OF THE CORRECT ANSWER IN THE SPACE AT THE RIGHT.*

1. Which one of the following statements about proper telephone usage is NOT always correct?
   When answering the telephone, you should
   A. know whom you are speaking to
   B. give the caller your undivided attention
   C. identify yourself to the caller
   D. obtain the information the caller wishes before you do your other work

   1.____

2. Assume that, as a member of a worker's safety committee in your agency, you are responsible for encouraging other employees to follow correct safety practices. While you are working on your regular assignment, you observe an employee violating a safety rule.
   Of the following, the BEST action for you to take FIRST is to
   A. speak to the employee about safety practices and order him to stop violating the safety rule
   B. speak to the employee about safety practices and point out the safety rule he is violating
   C. bring the matter up in the next committee meeting
   D. report this violation of the safety rule to the employee's supervisor

   2.____

3. Assume that you have been temporarily assigned by your supervisor to do a job which you do not want to do.
   The BEST action for you to take is to
   A. discuss the job with your supervisor, explaining why you do not want to do it
   B. discuss the job with your supervisor and tell her that you will not do it
   C. ask a co-worker to take your place on this job
   D. do some other job that you like; your supervisor may give the job you do not like to someone else

   3.____

4. Assume that you keep the confidential personnel files of employees in your unit. A friend asks you to obtain some information from the file of one of your co-workers.
   The BEST action to take is to _____ to your friend.
   A. ask the co-worker if you can give the information
   B. ask your supervisor if you can give the information
   C. give the information
   D. refuse to give the information

   4.____

Questions 5-8.

DIRECTIONS: Questions 5 through 8 are to be answered SOLELY on the basis of the information contained in the following passage.

City government is committed to providing a safe and healthy work environment for all city employees. An effective agency safety program reduces accidents by educating employees about the types of careless acts which can cause accidents. Even in an office, accidents can happen. If each employee is aware of possible safety hazards, the number of accidents on the job can be reduced.

Careless use of office equipment can cause accidents and injuries. For example, file cabinet drawers which are filled with papers can be so heavy that the entire cabinet could tip over from the weight of one open drawer.

The bottom drawers of desks and file cabinets should never be left open since employees can easily trip over open drawers and injure themselves.

When reaching for objects on a high shelf, an employee should use a strong, sturdy object such as a stepstool to stand on. Makeshift platforms made out of books, papers, or boxes can easily collapse. Even chairs can slide out from under foot, causing serious injury.

Even at an employee's desk, safety hazards can occur. Frayed or cut wires should be repaired or replaced immediately. Computers which are not firmly anchored to the desk or table could fall, causing injury.

Smoking is one of the major causes of fires in the office. A lighted match or improperly extinguished cigarette thrown into a wastebasket filled with paper could cause a major fire with possible loss of life. Where smoking is permitted, ashtrays should be used. Smoking is particularly dangerous in offices were flammable chemicals are used.

5. The goal of an effective safety program is to
   A. reduce office accidents
   B. stop employees from smoking on the job
   C. encourage employees to continue their education
   D. eliminate high shelves in offices

6. Desks and file cabinets can become safety hazards when
   A. their drawers are left open
   B. they are used as wastebaskets
   C. they are makeshift
   D. they are not anchored securely to the floor

7. Smoking is especially hazardous when it occurs
   A. near exposed wires
   B. in a crowded office
   C. in an area where flammable chemicals are used
   D. where books and papers are stored

8. Accidents are likely to occur when
   A. employees' desks are cluttered with books and papers
   B. employees are not aware of safety hazards
   C. employees close desk drawers
   D. stepstools are used to reach high objects

9. Assume that part of your job as a worker in the accounting division of a city agency is to answer the telephone.
   When you first answer the telephone, it is LEAST important to tell the caller
   A. your title
   B. your name
   C. the name of your unit
   D. the name of your agency

10. Assume that you are assigned to work as a receptionist, and your duties are to answer phones, greet visitors, and do other general office work. You are busy with a routine job when several visitors approach your desk.
    The BEST action to take is to
    A. ask the visitors to have a seat and assist them after your work is completed
    B. tell the visitors that you are busy and they should return at a more convenient time
    C. stop working long enough to assist the visitors
    D. continue working and wait for the visitors to ask you for assistance

11. Assume that your supervisor has chosen you to take a special course during hours to learn a new payroll procedure. Although you know that you were chosen because of your good work record, a co-worker, who feels that he should have been chosen, has been telling everyone in your unit that the choice was unfair.
    Of the following, the BEST way to handle this situation FIRST is to
    A. suggest to the co-worker that everything in life is unfair
    B. contact your union representative in case your co-worker presents a formal grievance
    C. tell your supervisor about your co-worker's complaints and let her handle the situation
    D. tell the co-worker that you were chosen because of your superior work record

12. Assume that while you are working on an assignment which must be completed quickly, a supervisor from another unit asks you to obtain information for her.
    Of the following, the BEST way to respond to her request is to
    A. tell her to return in an hour since you are busy
    B. give her the names of some people in her own unit who could help her
    C. tell her you are busy and refer her to a co-worker
    D. tell her that you are busy and ask her if she could wait until you finish your assignment

13. A co-worker in your unit is often off from work because of illness. Your supervisor assigns the co-worker's work to you when she is not there. Lately, doing her work has interfered with your own job.
    The BEST action for you to take FIRST is to
    A. discuss the problem with your supervisor
    B. complete your own work before starting your co-worker's work
    C. ask other workers in your unit to assist you
    D. work late in order to get the jobs done

14. During the month of June, 40,587 people attended a city-owned swimming pool. In July, 13,014 more people attended the swimming pool than the number that had attended in June. In August, 39,655 people attended the swimming pool. The TOTAL number of people who attended the swimming pool during the months of June, July, and August was 14._____
 A. 80,242 B. 93,256 C. 133,843 D. 210,382

Questions 15-22.

DIRECTIONS: Questions 15 through 22 test how well you understand what you read. It will be necessary for you to read carefully because your answers to these questions must be based ONLY on the information in the following paragraphs.

The telephone directory is made up of two books. The first book consists of the introductory section and the alphabetical listing of names section. The second book is the classified directory (also known as the yellow pages). Many people who are familiar with one book do not realize how useful the other can be. The efficient office worker should become familiar with both books in order to make the best use of this important source of information.

The introductory section gives general instructions for finding numbers in the alphabetical listing and classified directory. This section also explains how to use the telephone company's many services, including the operator and information services, gives examples of charges for local and long-distance calls, and lists area codes for the entire country. In addition, this section provides a useful zip code map.

The alphabetical listing of names section lists the names, addresses, and telephone numbers of subscribers in an area. Guide names, or *telltales*, are on the top corner of each page. These guide names indicate the first and last name to be found on that page. *Telltales* help locate any particular name quickly. A cross-reference spelling is also given to help locate names which are spelled several different ways. City, state, and federal government agencies are listed under the major government heading. For example, an agency of the federal government would be listed under *United States Government*.

The classified directory, or yellow pages, is a separate book. In this section are advertising services, public transportation line maps, shopping guides, and listings of businesses arranged by the type of product or services they offer. This book is most useful when looking for the name or phone number of a business when all that is known is the type of product offered and the address, or when trying to locate a particular type of business in an area. Businesses listed in the classified directory can usually be found in the alphabetical listing of names section. When the name of the business is known, you will find the address or phone number more quickly in the alphabetical listing of names section.

15. The introductory section provides 15._____
 A. shopping guides B. government listings
 C. business listings D. information services

16. Advertising services would be found in the 16._____
 A. introductory section B. alphabetical listing of names section\
 C. classified directory D. information services

17. According to the information in the above passage for locating government agencies, the Information Office of the Department of Consumer Affairs of New York City government would be alphabetically listed FIRST under
    A. *I* for Information Offices
    B. *D* for Department of Consumer Affairs
    C. *N* for New York City
    D. *G* for government

18. When the name of a business is known, the QUICKEST way to find the phone number is to look in the
    A. classified directory
    B. introductory section
    C. alphabetical listing of name section
    D. advertising service section

19. The QUICKEST way to find the phone number of a business when the type of service a business offers and its address is known is to look in the
    A. classified directory
    B. alphabetical listing of names section
    C. introductory section
    D. information service

20. What is a *telltale*?
    A. An alphabetical listing
    B. A guide name
    C. A map
    D. A cross-reference listing

21. The BEST way to find a postal zip code is to look in the
    A. classified directory
    B. introductory section
    C. alphabetical listing of names section
    D. government heading

22. To help find names which have several different spellings, the telephone directory provides
    A. cross-reference spelling
    B. *telltales*
    C. spelling guides
    D. advertising services

23. Assume that your agency has been given $2,025 to purchase file cabinets. If each file cabinet costs $135, how many file cabinet can your agency purchase?
    A. 8   B. 10   C. 15   D. 16

24. Assume that your unit ordered 14 staplers at a total cost of $30.20 and each stapler cost the same.
    The cost of one stapler was MOST NEARLY
    A. $1.02   B. $1.61   C. $2.16   D. $2.26

25. Assume that you are responsible for counting and recording licensing fees collected by your department. On a particular day, your department collected in fees 40 checks in the amount of $6 each, 80 checks in the amount of $4 each, 45 twenty dollar bills, 30 ten dollar bills, 42 five dollar bills, and 186 one dollar bills.
The TOTAL amount in fees collected on that day was
    A. $1,406 B. $1,706 C. $2,156 D. $2,356

26. Assume that you are responsible for your agency's petty cash fund. During the month of February, you pay out 7 $2.00 subway fares and one taxi fare for $10.85. You pay out nothing else from the fund. At the end of February, you count the money left in the fund and find 3 one dollar bills, 4 quarters, 5 dimes, and 4 nickels.
The amount of money you had available in the petty cash fund at the BEGINNING of February was
    A. $4.70 B. $16.35 C. $24.85 D. $29.55

27. You overhear your supervisor criticize a co-worker for handling equipment in an unsafe way. You feel that the criticism may be unfair.
Of the following, it would be BEST for you to
    A. take your co-worker aside and tell her how you feel about your supervisor's comments
    B. interrupt the discussion and defend your co-worker to your supervisor
    C. continue working as if you had not overheard the discussion
    D. make a list of other workers who have violated safety rules and give it to your supervisor

28. Assume that you have been assigned to work on a long-term project with an employee who is known for being uncooperative.
In beginning to work with this employee, it would be LEAST desirable for you to
    A. understand why the person is uncooperative
    B. act in a calm manner rather than an emotional manner
    C. be appreciative of the co-worker's work
    D. report the co-worker's lack of cooperation to your supervisor

29. Assume that you are assigned to sell tickets at a city-owned ice skating rink. An adult ticket costs $4.50, and a children's ticket costs $2.25. At the end of a day, you find that you have sold 36 adult tickets and 80 children's tickets.
The TOTAL amount of money you collected for that day was
    A. $244.80 B. $318.00 C. $342.00 D. $348.00

30. If each office worker files 487 index cards in one hour, how many card can 26 office workers file in one hour?
    A. 10,662 B. 12,175 C. 12,662 D. 14,266

KEY (CORRECT ANSWERS)

1.	D	11.	C	21.	B
2.	B	12.	D	22.	A
3.	A	13.	A	23.	C
4.	D	14.	C	24.	C
5.	A	15.	D	25.	C
6.	A	16.	C	26.	D
7.	C	17.	C	27.	C
8.	B	18.	C	28.	D
9.	A	19.	A	29.	C
10.	C	20.	B	30.	C

READING COMPREHENSION
UNDERSTANDING AND INTERPRETING WRITTEN MATERIAL
EXAMINATION SECTION
TEST 1

DIRECTIONS: Each question or incomplete statement is followed by several suggested answers or completions. Select the one that BEST answers the question or completes the statement. *PRINT THE LETTER OF THE CORRECT ANSWER IN THE SPACE AT THE RIGHT.*

Questions 1-3.

DIRECTIONS: Questions 1 through 3 are to be answered SOLELY on the basis of the following statement.

The equipment in a mailroom may include a mail metering machine. This machine simultaneously stamps, postmarks, seals, and counts letters as fast as the operator can feed them. It can also print the proper postage directly on a gummed strip to be affixed to bulky items. It is equipped with a meter which is removed from the machine and sent to the postmaster to be set for a given number of stampings of any denomination. The setting of the meter must be paid for in advance. One of the advantages of metered mail is that it bypasses the cancellation operation and thereby facilitates handling by the post office. Mail metering also makes the pilfering of stamps impossible, but does not prevent the passage of personal mail in company envelopes through the meters unless there is established a rigid control or censorship over outgoing mail.

1. According to this statement, the postmaster

   A. is responsible for training new clerks in the use of mail metering machines
   B. usually recommends that both large and small firms adopt the use of mail metering machines
   C. is responsible for setting the meter to print a fixed number of stampings
   D. examines the mail metering machine to see that they are properly installed in the mailroom

2. According to this statement, the use of mail metering machines

   A. requires the employment of more clerks in a mailroom than does the use of postage stamps
   B. interferes with the handling of large quantities of outgoing mail
   C. does not prevent employees from sending their personal letters at company expense
   D. usually involves smaller expenditures for mailroom equipment than does the use of postage stamps

3. On the basis of this statement, it is MOST accurate to state that

   A. mail metering machines are often used for opening envelopes
   B. postage stamps are generally used when bulky packages are to be mailed
   C. the use of metered mail tends to interfere with rapid mail handling by the post office
   D. mail metering machines can seal and count letters at the same time

Questions 4-5.

DIRECTIONS: Questions 4 and 5 are to be answered SOLELY on the basis of the following statement.

Forms are printed sheets of paper on which information is to be entered. While what is printed on the form is most important, the kind of paper used in making the form is also important. The kind of paper should be selected with regard to the use to which the form will be subjected. Printing a form on an unnecessarily expensive grade of papers is wasteful. On the other hand, using too cheap or flimsy a form can materially interfere with satisfactory performance of the work the form is being planned to do. Thus, a form printed on both sides normally requires a heavier paper than a form printed only on one side. Forms to be used as permanent records, or which are expected to have a very long life in files, requires a quality of paper which will not disintegrate or discolor with age. A form which will go through a great deal of handling requires a strong, tough paper, while thinness is a necessary qualification where the making of several copies of a form will be required.

4. According to this statement, the type of paper used for making forms

    A. should be chosen in accordance with the use to which the form will be put
    B. should be chosen before the type of printing to be used has been decided upon
    C. is as important as the information which is printed on it
    D. should be strong enough to be used for any purpose

5. According to this statement, forms that are

    A. printed on both sides are usually economical and desirable
    B. to be filed permanently should not deteriorate as time goes on
    C. expected to last for a long time should be handled carefully
    D. to be filed should not be printed on inexpensive paper

Questions 6-8.

DIRECTIONS: Questions 6 through 8 are to be answered SOLELY on the basis of the following paragraph.

The increase in the number of public documents in the last two centuries closely matches the increase in population in the United States. The great number of public documents has become a serious threat to their usefulness. It is necessary to have programs which will reduce the number of public documents that are kept and which will, at the same time, assure keeping those that have value. Such programs need a great deal of thought to have any success.

6. According to the above paragraph, public documents may be LESS useful if

    A. the files are open to the public
    B. the record room is too small
    C. the copying machine is operated only during normal working hours
    D. too many records are being kept

7. According to the above paragraph, the growth of the population in the United States has matched the growth in the quantity of public documents for a period of MOST NEARLY _____ years.

    A. 50 B. 100 C. 200 D. 300

8. According to the above paragraph, the increased number of public documents has made it necessary to

    A. find out which public documents are worth keeping
    B. reduce the great number of public documents by decreasing government services
    C. eliminate the copying of all original public documents
    D. avoid all new copying devices

Questions 9-10.

DIRECTIONS: Questions 9 and 10 are to be answered SOLELY on the basis of the following paragraph.

The work goals of an agency can best be reached if the employees understand and agree with these goals. One way to gain such understanding and agreement is for management to encourage and seriously consider suggestions from employees in the setting of agency goals.

9. On the basis of the above paragraph, the BEST way to achieve the work goals of an agency is to

    A. make certain that employees work as hard as possible
    B. study the organizational structure of the agency
    C. encourage employees to think seriously about the agency's problems
    D. stimulate employee understanding of the work goals

10. On the basis of the above paragraph, understanding and agreement with agency goals can be gained by

    A. allowing the employees to set agency goals
    B. reaching agency goals quickly
    C. legislative review of agency operations
    D. employee participation in setting agency goals

Questions 11-13.

DIRECTIONS: Questions 11 through 13 are to be answered SOLELY on the basis of the following paragraph.

In order to organize records properly, it is necessary to start from their very beginning and trace each copy of the record to find out how it is used, how long it is used, and what may finally be done with it. Although several copies of the record are made, one copy should be marked as the copy of record. This is the formal legal copy, held to meet the requirements of the law. The other copies may be retained for brief periods for reference purposes, but these copies should not be kept after their usefulness as reference ends. There is another reason for tracing records through the office and that is to determine how long it takes the copy of record to reach the central file. The copy of record must not be kept longer than necessary by the section of the office which has prepared it, but should be sent to the central file as soon as possible so that it can be available to the various sections of the office. The central file can make the copy of record available to the various sections of the office at an early date only if it arrives at the central file as quickly as possible. Just as soon as its immediate or active service period is ended, the copy of record should be removed from the central file and put into the inactive file in the office to be stored for whatever length of time may be necessary to meet legal requirements, and then destroyed.

11. According to the above paragraph, a reason for tracing records through an office is to

    A. determine how long the central file must keep the records
    B. organize records properly
    C. find out how many copies of each record are required
    D. identify the copy of record

12. According to the above paragraph, in order for the central file to have the copy of record available as soon as possible for the various sections of the office, it is MOST important that the

    A. copy of record to be sent to the central file meets the requirements of the law
    B. copy of record is not kept in the inactive file too long
    C. section preparing the copy of record does not unduly delay in sending it to the central file
    D. central file does not keep the copy of record beyond its active service period

13. According to the above paragraph, the length of time a copy of a record is kept in the inactive file of an office depends CHIEFLY on the

    A. requirements of the law
    B. length of time that is required to trace the copy of record through the office
    C. use that is made of the copy of record
    D. length of the period that the copy of record is used for reference purposes

Questions 14-16.

DIRECTIONS: Questions 14 through 16 are to be answered SOLELY on the basis of the following paragraph.

The office was once considered as nothing more than a focal point of internal and external correspondence. It was capable only of dispatching a few letters upon occasion and of preparing records of little practical value. Under such a concept, the vitality of the office force was impaired. Initiative became stagnant, and the lot of the office worker was not likely to be a happy one. However, under the new concept of office management, the possibilities of waste and mismanagement in office operation are now fully recognized, as are the possibilities for the modern office to assist in the direction and control of business operations. Fortunately, the modern concept of the office as a centralized service-rendering unit is gaining ever greater acceptance in today's complex business world, for without the modern office, the production wheels do not turn and the distribution of goods and services is not possible.

14. According to the above paragraph, the fundamental difference between the old and the new concept of the office is the change in the

    A. accepted functions of the office
    B. content and the value of the records kept
    C. office methods and systems
    D. vitality and morale of the office force

14.____

15. According to the above paragraph, an office operated today under the old concept of the office MOST likely would

    A. make older workers happy in their jobs
    B. be part of an old thriving business concern
    C. have a passive role in the conduct of a business enterprise
    D. attract workers who do not believe in modern methods

15.____

16. Of the following, the MOST important implication of the above paragraph is that a present-day business organization cannot function effectively without the

    A. use of modern office equipment
    B. participation and cooperation of the office
    C. continued modernization of office procedures
    D. employment of office workers with skill and initiative

16.____

Questions 17-20.

DIRECTIONS: Questions 17 through 20 are to be answered SOLELY on the basis of the following paragraph.

   A report is frequently ineffective because the person writing it is not fully acquainted with all the necessary details before he actually starts to construct the report. All details pertaining to the subject should be known before the report is started. If the essential facts are not known, they should be investigated. It is wise to have essential facts written down rather than to depend too much on memory, especially if the facts pertain to such matters as amounts, dates, names of persons, or other specific data. When the necessary information has been gathered, the general plan and content of the report should be thought out before the writing is actually begun. A person with little or no experience in writing reports may find that it is wise to make a brief outline. Persons with more experience should not need a written outline, but they should make mental notes of the steps they are to follow. If writing reports without dictation is a regular part of an office worker's duties, he should set aside a certain time during the day when he is least likely to be interrupted. That may be difficult, but in most offices there are certain times in the day when the callers, telephone calls, and other interruptions are not numerous. During those times, it is best to write reports that need undivided concentration. Reports that are written amid a series of interruptions may be poorly done.

17. Before starting to write an effective report, it is necessary to

    A. memorize all specific information
    B. disregard ambiguous data
    C. know all pertinent information
    D. develop a general plan

17.____

18. Reports dealing with complex and difficult material should be

   A. prepared and written by the supervisor of the unit
   B. written when there is the least chance of interruption
   C. prepared and written as part of regular office routine
   D. outlined and then dictated

19. According to the paragraph, employees with no prior familiarity in writing reports may find it helpful to

   A. prepare a brief outline
   B. mentally prepare a synopsis of the report's content
   C. have a fellow employee help in writing the report
   D. consult previous reports

20. In writing a report, needed information which is unclear should be

   A. disregarded   B. memorized
   C. investigated   D. gathered

Questions 21-25.

DIRECTIONS: Questions 21 through 25 are to be answered SOLELY on the basis of the following passage.

Positive discipline minimizes the amount of personal supervision required and aids in the maintenance of standards. When a new employee has been properly introduced and carefully instructed, when he has come to know the supervisor and has confidence in the supervisor's ability to take care of him, when he willingly cooperates with the supervisor, that employee has been under positive discipline and can be put on his own to produce the quantity and quality of work desired. Negative discipline, the fear of transfer to a less desirable location, for example, to a limited extent may restrain certain individuals from overt violation of rules and regulations governing attendance and conduct which in governmental agencies are usually on at least an agency-wide basis. Negative discipline may prompt employees to perform according to certain rules to avoid a penalty such as, for example, docking for tardiness.

21. According to the above passage, it is reasonable to assume that in the area of discipline, the first-line supervisor in a governmental agency has GREATER scope for action in

   A. *positive* discipline, because negative discipline is largely taken care of by agency rules and regulations
   B. *negative* discipline, because rules and procedures are already fixed and the supervisor can rely on them
   C. *positive* discipline, because the supervisor is in a position to recommend transfers
   D. *negative* discipline, because positive discipline is reserved for people on a higher supervisory level

22. In order to maintain positive discipline of employees under his supervision, it is MOST important for a supervisor to

   A. assure each employee that he has nothing to worry about
   B. insist at the outset on complete cooperation from employees

C. be sure that each employee is well trained in his job
D. inform new employees of the penalties for not meeting standards

23. According to the above passage, a feature of negative discipline is that it   23.____

    A. may lower employee morale
    B. may restrain employees from disobeying the rules
    C. censures equal treatment of employees
    D. tends to create standards for quality of work

24. A REASONABLE conclusion based on the above passage is that positive discipline benefits a supervisor because   24.____

    A. he can turn over orientation and supervision of a new employee to one of his subordinates
    B. subordinates learn to cooperate with one another when working on an assignment
    C. it is easier to administer
    D. it cuts down, in the long run, on the amount of time the supervisor needs to spend on direct supervision

25. Based on the above passage, it is REASONABLE to assume, that an important difference between positive discipline and negative discipline is that positive discipline   25.____

    A. is concerned with the quality of work and negative discipline with the quantity of work
    B. leads to a more desirable basis for motivation of the employee
    C. is more likely to be concerned with agency rules and regulations
    D. uses fear while negative discipline uses penalties to prod employees to adequate performance

KEY (CORRECT ANSWERS)

1.	C	11.	B
2.	C	12.	C
3.	D	13.	A
4.	A	14.	A
5.	B	15.	C
6.	D	16.	B
7.	C	17.	C
8.	A	18.	B
9.	D	19.	A
10.	D	20.	B

21. A
22. C
23. B
24. D
25. B

TEST 2

Questions 1-6.

DIRECTIONS: Questions 1 through 6 are to be answered SOLELY on the basis of the following passage.

Inherent in all organized endeavors is the need to resolve the individual differences involved in conflict. Conflict may be either a positive or negative factor since it may lead to creativity, innovation and progress on the one hand, or it may result, on the other hand, in a deterioration or even destruction of the organization. Thus, some forms of conflict are desirable, whereas others are undesirable and ethically wrong.

There are three management strategies which deal with interpersonal conflict. In the *divide-and-rule strategy*, management attempts to maintain control by limiting the conflict to those directly involved and preventing their disagreement from spreading to the larger group. The *suppression-of-differences strategy* entails ignoring conflicts or pretending they are irrelevant. In the *working-through-differences strategy*, management actively attempts to solve or resolve intergroup or interpersonal conflicts. Of the three strategies, only the last directly attacks and has the potential for eliminating the causes of conflict. An essential part of this strategy, however, is its employment by a committed and relatively mature management team.

1. According to the above passage, the *divide-and-rule strategy tor* dealing with conflict is the attempt to

    A. involve other people in the conflict
    B. restrict the conflict to those participating in it
    C. divide the conflict into positive and negative factors
    D. divide the conflict into a number of smaller ones

2. The word *conflict* is used in relation to both positive and negative factors in this passage. Which one of the following words is MOST likely to describe the activity which the word *conflict,* in the sense of the passage, implies?

    A. Competition   B. Confusion
    C. Cooperation   D. Aggression

3. According to the above passage, which one of the following characteristics is shared by both the *suppression-of-differences strategy* and the *divide-and-rule strategy*?

    A. Pretending that conflicts are irrelevant
    B. Preventing conflicts from spreading to the group situation
    C. Failure to directly attack the causes of conflict
    D. Actively attempting to resolve interpersonal conflict

4. According to the above passage, the successful resolution of interpersonal conflict requires

    A. allowing the group to mediate conflicts between two individuals
    B. division of the conflict into positive and negative factors
    C. involvement of a committed, mature management team
    D. ignoring minor conflicts until they threaten the organization

5. Which can be MOST reasonably inferred from the above passage? Conflict between two individuals is LEAST likely to continue when management uses

    A. the *working-through differences strategy*
    B. the *suppression-of differences strategy*
    C. the *divide-and-rule strategy*
    D. a combination of all three strategies

6. According to the above passage, a DESIRABLE result of conflict in an organization is when conflict

    A. exposes production problems in the organization
    B. can be easily ignored by management
    C. results in advancement of more efficient managers
    D. leads to development of new methods

Questions 7-13.

DIRECTIONS: Questions 7 through 13 are to be answered SOLELY on the basis of the passage below.

Modern management places great emphasis on the concept of communication. The communication process consists of the steps through which an idea or concept passes from its inception by one person, the sender, until it is acted upon by another person, the receiver. Through an understanding of these steps and some of the possible barriers that may occur, more effective communication may be achieved. The first step in the communication process is ideation by the sender. This is the formation of the intended content of the message he wants to transmit. In the next step, encoding, the sender organizes his ideas into a series of symbols designed to communicate his message to his intended receiver. He selects suitable words or phrases that can be understood by the receiver, and he also selects the appropriate media to be used—for example, memorandum, conference, etc. The third step is transmission of the encoded message through selected channels in the organizational structure. In the fourth step, the receiver enters the process by tuning in to receive the message. If the receiver does not function, however, the message is lost. For example, if the message is oral, the receiver must be a good listener. The fifth step is decoding of the message by the receiver, as for example, by changing words into ideas. At this step, the decoded message may not be the same idea that the sender originally encoded because the sender and receiver have different perceptions regarding the meaning of certain words. Finally, the receiver acts or responds. He may file the information, ask for more information, or take other action. There can be no assurance, however, that communication has taken place unless there is some type of feedback to the sender in the form of an acknowledgement that the message was received.

7. According to the above passage, *ideation* is the process by which the

    A. sender develops the intended content of the message
    B. sender organizes his ideas into a series of symbols
    C. receiver tunes in to receive the message
    D. receiver decodes the message

8. In the last sentence of the passage, the word *feedback* refers to the process by which the sender is assured that the

   A. receiver filed the information
   B. receiver's perception is the same as his own
   C. message was received
   D. message was properly interpreted

9. Which one of the following BEST shows the order of the steps in the communication process as described in the passage?

   A. 1 - ideation   2 - encoding
      3 - decoding   4 - transmission
      5 - receiving   6 - action
      7 - feedback to the sender

   B. 1 - ideation   2 - encoding
      3 - transmission   4 - decoding
      5 - receiving   6 - action
      7 - feedback to the sender

   C. 1 - ideation   2 - decoding
      3 - transmission   4 - receiving
      5 - encoding   6 - action
      7 - feedback to the sender

   D. 1 - ideation   2 - encoding
      3 - transmission   4 - receiving
      5 - decoding   6 - action
      7 - feedback to the sender

10. Which one of the following BEST expresses the main theme of the passage?

    A. Different individuals have the same perceptions regarding the meaning of words.
    B. An understanding of the steps in the communication process may achieve better communication.
    C. Receivers play a passive role in the communication process.
    D. Senders should not communicate with receivers who transmit feedback.

11. The above passage implies that a receiver does NOT function properly when he

    A. transmits feedback   B. files the information
    C. is a poor listener   D. asks for more information

12. Which one of the following, according to the above passage, is included in the SECOND step of the communication process?

    A. Selecting the appropriate media to be used in transmission
    B. Formulation of the intended content of the message
    C. Using appropriate media to respond to the receiver's feedback
    D. Transmitting the message through selected channels in the organization

13. The above passage implies that the *decoding process* is MOST NEARLY the reverse of the _____ process.

    A. transmission   B. receiving
    C. feedback   D. encoding

Questions 14-19.

DIRECTIONS: Questions 14 through 19 are to be answered SOLELY on the basis of the following passage.

It is often said that no system will work if the people who carry it out do not want it to work. In too many cases, a departmental reorganization that seemed technically sound and economically practical has proved to be a failure because the planners neglected to take the human factor into account. The truth is that employees are likely to feel threatened when they learn that a major change is in the wind. It does not matter whether or not the change actually poses a threat to an employee; the fact that he believes it does or fears it might is enough to make him feel insecure. Among the dangers he fears, the foremost is the possibility that his job may cease to exist and that he may be laid off or shunted into a less skilled position at lower pay. Even if he knows that his own job category is secure, however, he is likely to fear losing some of the important intangible advantages of his present position—for instance, he may fear that he will be separated from his present companions and thrust in with a group of strangers, or that he will find himself in a lower position on the organizational ladder if a new position is created above his.

It is important that management recognize these natural fears and take them into account in planning any kind of major change. While there is no cut-and-dried formula for preventing employee resistance, there are several steps that can be taken to reduce employees' fears and gain their cooperation. First, unwarranted fears can be dispelled if employees are kept informed of the planning from the start and if they know exactly what to expect. Next, assurance on matters such as retraining, transfers, and placement help should be given as soon as it is clear what direction the reorganization will take. Finally, employees' participation in the planning should be actively sought. There is a great psychological difference between feeling that a change is being forced upon one from the outside, and feeling that one is an insider who is helping to bring about a change.

14. According to the above passage, employees who are not in real danger of losing their jobs because of a proposed reorganization

    A. will be eager to assist in the reorganization
    B. will pay little attention to the reorganization
    C. should not be taken into account in planning the reorganization
    D. are nonetheless likely to feel threatened by the reorganization

15. The passage mentions the *intangible advantages* of a position.
    Which of the following BEST describes the kind of advantages alluded to in the passage?

    A. Benefits such as paid holidays and vacations
    B. Satisfaction of human needs for things like friendship and status
    C. Qualities such as leadership and responsibility
    D. A work environment that meets satisfactory standards of health and safety

16. According to the passage, an employee's fear that a reorganization may separate him from his present companions is a (n)

    A. childish and immature reaction to change
    B. unrealistic feeling since this is not going to happen

C. possible reaction that the planners should be aware of
D. incentive to employees to participate in the planning

17. On the basis of the above passage, it would be DESIRABLE, when planning a departmental reorganization, to

    A. be governed by employee feelings and attitudes
    B. give some employees lower positions
    C. keep employees informed
    D. lay off those who are less skilled

18. What does the passage say can be done to help gain employees' cooperation in a reorganization?

    A. Making sure that the change is technically sound, that it is economically practical, and that the human factor is taken into account
    B. Keeping employees fully informed, offering help in fitting them into new positions, and seeking their participation in the planning
    C. Assuring employees that they will not be laid off, that they will not be reassigned to a group of strangers, and that no new positions will be created on the organization ladder
    D. Reducing employees' fears, arranging a retraining program, and providing for transfers

19. Which of the following suggested titles would be MOST appropriate for this passage?

    A. PLANNING A DEPARTMENTAL REORGANIZATION
    B. WHY EMPLOYEES ARE AFRAID
    C. LOOKING AHEAD TO THE FUTURE
    D. PLANNING FOR CHANGE: THE HUMAN FACTOR

Questions 20-22.

DIRECTIONS: Questions 20 through 22 are to be answered SOLELY on the basis of the following passage.

The achievement of good human relations is essential if a business office is to produce at top efficiency and is to be a pleasant place in which to work. All office workers plan an important role in handling problems in human relations. They should, therefore, strive to acquire the understanding, tactfulness, and awareness necessary to deal effectively with actual office situations involving co-workers on all levels. Only in this way can they truly become responsible, interested, cooperative, and helpful members of the staff.

20. The selection implies that the MOST important value of good human relations in an office is to develop

    A. efficiency   B. cooperativeness
    C. tact   D. pleasantness and efficiency

21. Office workers should acquire understanding in dealing with

    A. co-workers   B. subordinates
    C. superiors   D. all members of the staff

22. The selection indicates that a highly competent secretary who is also very argumentative is meeting office requirements

    A. wholly
    B. partly
    C. slightly
    D. not at all

Questions 23-25.

DIRECTIONS: Questions 23 through 25 are to be answered SOLELY on the basis of the following passage.

It is common knowledge that ability to do a particular job and performance on the job do not always go hand in hand. Persons with great potential abilities sometimes fall down on the job because of laziness or lack of interest in the job, while persons with mediocre talents have often achieved excellent results through their industry and their loyalty to the interests of their employers. It is clear; therefore, that in a balanced personnel program, measures of employee ability need to be supplemented by measures of employee performance, for the final test of any employee is his performance on the job.

23. The MOST accurate of the following statements, on the basis of the above paragraph, is that

    A. employees who lack ability are usually not industrious
    B. an employee's attitudes are more important than his abilities
    C. mediocre employees who are interested in their work are preferable to employees who possess great ability
    D. superior capacity for performance should be supplemented with proper attitudes

24. On the basis of the above paragraph, the employee of most value to his employer is NOT necessarily the one who

    A. best understands the significance of his duties
    B. achieves excellent results
    C. possesses the greatest talents
    D. produces the greatest amount of work

25. According to the above paragraph, an employee's efficiency is BEST determined by an

    A. appraisal of his interest in his work
    B. evaluation of the work performed by him
    C. appraisal of his loyalty to his employer
    D. evaluation of his potential ability to perform his work

KEY (CORRECT ANSWERS)

1. B
2. A
3. C
4. C
5. A

6. D
7. A
8. C
9. D
10. B

11. C
12. A
13. D
14. D
15. B

16. C
17. C
18. B
19. D
20. D

21. D
22. B
23. D
24. C
25. B

TEST 3

Questions 1-8.

DIRECTIONS: Questions 1 through 8 are to be answered SOLELY on the basis of the following information and directions.

Assume that you are a clerk in a city agency. Your supervisor has asked you to classify each of the accidents that happened to employees in the agency into the following five categories:

   A. An accident that occurred in the period from January through June, between 9 A.M. and 12 Noon, that was the result of carelessness on the part of the injured employee, that caused the employee to lose less than seven working hours, that happened to an employee who was 40 years of age or over, and who was employed in the agency for less than three years;

   B. An accident that occurred in the period from July through December, after 1 P.M., that was the result of unsafe conditions, that caused the injured employee to lose less than seven working hours, that happened to an employee who was 40 years of age or over, and who was employed in the agency for three years or more;

   C. An accident that occurred in the period from January through June, after 1 P.M., that was the result of carelessness on the part of the injured employee, that caused the injured employee to lose seven or more working hours, that happened to an employee who was less than 40 years old, and who was employed in the agency for three years or more;

   D. An accident that occurred in the period from July through December, between 9 A.M. and 12 Noon, that was the result of unsafe conditions, that caused the injured employee to lose seven or more working hours, that happened to an employee who was less than 40 years old, and who was employed in the agency for less than three years;

   E. Accidents that cannot be classified in any of the foregoing groups. NOTE: In classifying these accidents, an employee's age and length of service are computed as of the date of accident. In all cases, it is to be assumed that each employee has been employed continuously in city service, and that each employee works seven hours a day, from 9 A.M. to 5 P.M., with lunch from 12 Noon to 1 P.M. In each question, consider only the information which will assist you in classifying the accident. Any information which is of no assistance in classifying an accident should not be considered.

1. The unsafe condition of the stairs in the building caused Miss Perkins to have an accident on October 14, 2003 at 4 P.M. When she returned to work the following day at 1 P.M., Miss Perkins said that the accident was the first one that had occurred to her in her ten years of employment with the agency. She was born on April 27, 1962.

2. On the day after she completed her six-month probationary period of employment with the agency, Miss Green, who had been considered a careful worker by her supervisor, injured her left foot in an accident caused by her own carelessness. She went home immediately after the accident, which occurred at 10 A.M., March 19, 2004, but returned to work at the regular time on the following morning. Miss Green was born July 12, 1963 in New York City.

3. The unsafe condition of a duplicating machine caused Mr. Martin to injure himself in an accident on September 8, 2006 at 2 P.M. As a result of the accident, he was unable to work the remainder of the day, but returned to his office ready for work on the following morning. Mr. Martin, who has been working for the agency since April 1, 2003, was born in St. Louis on February 1, 1968.

3.____

4. Mr. Smith was hospitalized for two weeks because of a back injury resulted from an accident on the morning of November 16, 2006. Investigation of the accident revealed that it was caused by the unsafe condition of the floor on which Mr. Smith had been walking. Mr. Smith, who is an accountant, has been an employee of the agency since March 1, 2004, and was born in Ohio on June 10, 1968.

4.____

5. Mr. Allen cut his right hand because he was careless in operating a multilith machine. Mr. Allen, who was 33 years old when the accident took place, has been employed by the agency since August 17, 1992. The accident, which occurred on January 26, 2006, at 2 P.M., caused Mr. Allen to be absent from work for the rest of the day. He was able to return to work the next morning.

5.____

6. Mr. Rand, who is a college graduate, was born on December, 28, 1967, and has been working for the agency since January 7, 2002. On Monday, April 25, 2005, at 2 P.M., his carelessness in operating a duplicating machine caused him to have an accident and to be sent home from work immediately. Fortunately, he was able to return to work at his regular time on the following Wednesday.

6.____

7. Because he was careless in running down a flight of stairs, Mr. Brown fell, bruising his right hand. Although the accident occurred shortly after he arrived for work on the morning of May 22, 2006, he was unable to resume work until 3 P.M. that day. Mr. Brown was born on August 15, 1966, and began working for the agency on September 12, 2003, as a clerk, at a salary of $22,750 per annum.

7.____

8. On December 5, 2005, four weeks after he had begun working for the agency, the unsafe condition of an automatic stapling machine caused Mr. Thomas to injure himself in an accident. Mr. Thomas, who was born on May 19, 1975, lost three working days because of the accident, which occurred at 11:45 A.M.

8.____

Questions 9-10.

DIRECTIONS: Questions 9 and 10 are to be answered SOLELY on the basis of the following paragraph.

An impending reorganization within an agency will mean loss by transfer of several professional staff members from the personnel division. The division chief is asked to designate the persons to be transferred. After reviewing the implications of this reduction of staff with his assistant, the division chief discusses the matter at a staff meeting. He adopts the recommendations of several staff members to have volunteers make up the required reduction.

9. The decision to permit personnel to volunteer for transfer is

   A. *poor;* it is not likely that the members of a division are of equal value to the division chief
   B. *good;* dissatisfied members will probably be more productive elsewhere
   C. *poor;* the division chief has abdicated his responsibility to carry out the order given to him
   D. *good;* morale among remaining staff is likely to improve in a more cohesive framework

10. Suppose that one of the volunteers is a recently appointed employee who has completed his probationary period acceptably, but whose attitude toward division operations and agency administration tends to be rather negative and sometimes even abrasive. Because of his lack of commitment to the division, his transfer is recommended. If the transfer is approved, the division chief should, prior to the transfer,

    A. discuss with the staff the importance of commitment to the work of the agency and its relationship with job satisfaction
    B. refrain from any discussion of attitude with the employee
    C. discuss with the employee his concern about the employee's attitude
    D. avoid mention of attitude in the evaluation appraisal prepared for the receiving division chief

Questions 11-16.

DIRECTIONS: Questions 11 through 16 are to be answered SOLELY on the basis of the following paragraph.

Methods of administration of office activities, much of which consists of providing information and *know-how* needed to coordinate both activities within that particular office and other offices, have been among the last to come under the spotlight of management analysis. Progress has been rapid during the past decade, however, and is now accelerating at such a pace that an *information revolution* in office management appears to be in the making. Although triggered by technological breakthroughs in electronic computers and other giant steps in mechanization, this information revolution must be attributed to underlying forces, such as the increased complexity of both governmental and private enterprise, and ever-keener competition. Size, diversification, specialization of function, and decentralization are among the forces which make coordination of activities both more imperative and more difficult. Increased competition, both domestic and international, leaves little margin for error in managerial decisions. Several developments during recent years indicate an evolving pattern. In 1960, the American Management Association expanded the scope of its activities and changed the name of its Office Management Division to Administrative Services Division. Also in 1960, the magazine *Office Management* merged with the magazine *American Business,* and this new publication was named *Administrative Management.*

4 (#3)

11. A REASONABLE inference that can be made from the information in the above paragraph is that an important role of the office manager today is to

    A. work toward specialization of functions performed by his subordinates
    B. inform and train subordinates regarding any new developments in computer technology and mechanization
    C. assist the professional management analysts with the management analysis work in the organization
    D. supply information that can be used to help coordinate and manage the other activities of the organization

11.____

12. An IMPORTANT reason for the *information revolution* that has been taking place in office management is the

    A. advance made in management analysis in the past decade
    B. technological breakthrough in electronic computers and mechanization
    C. more competitive and complicated nature of private business and government
    D. increased efficiency of office management techniques in the past ten years

12.____

13. According to the above paragraph, specialization of function in an organization is MOST likely to result in

    A. the elimination of errors in managerial decisions
    B. greater need to coordinate activities
    C. more competition with other organizations, both domestic and international
    D. a need for office managers with greater flexibility

13.____

14. The word *evolving,* as used in the third from last sentence in the above paragraph, means MOST NEARLY

    A. developing by gradual changes
    B. passing on to others
    C. occurring periodically
    D. breaking up into separate, constituent parts

14.____

15. Of the following, the MOST reasonable implication of the changes in names mentioned in the last part of the above paragraph is that these groups are attempting to

    A. professionalize the field of office management and the title of Office Manager
    B. combine two publications into one because of the increased costs of labor and materials
    C. adjust to the fact that the field of office management is broadening
    D. appeal to the top managerial people rather than the office management people in business and government

15.____

16. According to the above paragraph, intense competition among domestic and international enterprises makes it MOST important for an organization's managerial staff to

    A. coordinate and administer office activities with other activities in the organization
    B. make as few errors in decision-making as possible
    C. concentrate on decentralization and reduction of size of the individual divisions of the organization
    D. restrict decision-making only to top management officials

16.____

Questions 17-21.

DIRECTIONS: Questions 17 through 21 are to be answered SOLELY on the basis of the following passage.

For some office workers, it is useful to be familiar with the four main classes of domestic mail; for others, it is essential. Each class has a different rate of postage, and some have requirements concerning wrapping, sealing, or special information to be placed on the package. First class mail, the class which may not be opened for postal inspection, includes letters, postcards, business reply cards, and other kinds of written matter. There are different rates for some of the kinds of cards which can be sent by first class mail. The maximum weight for an item sent by first class mail is 70 pounds. An item which is not letter size should be marked *First Class* on all sides. Although office workers most often come into contact with first class mail, they may find it helpful to know something about the other classes. Second class mail is generally used for mailing newspapers and magazines. Publishers of these articles must meet certain U.S. Postal Service requirements in order to obtain a permit to use second class mailing rates. Third class mail, which must weigh less than 1 pound, includes printed materials and merchandise parcels. There are two rate structures for this class - a single piece rate and a bulk rate. Fourth class mail, also known as parcel post, includes packages weighing from one to 40 pounds. For more information about these classes of mail and the actual mailing rates, contact your local post office.

17. According to this passage, first class mail is the *only* class which

    A. has a limit on the maximum weight of an item
    B. has different rates for items within the class
    C. may not be opened for postal inspection
    D. should be used by office workers

17.____

18. According to this passage, the one of the following items which may CORRECTLY be sent by fourth class mail is a

    A. magazine weighing one-half pound
    B. package weighing one-half pound
    C. package weighing two pounds
    D. postcard

18.____

19. According to this passage, there are different postage rates for

    A. a newspaper sent by second class mail and a magazine sent by second class mail
    B. each of the classes of mail
    C. each pound of fourth class mail
    D. printed material sent by third class mail and merchandise parcels sent by third class mail

19.____

20. In order to send a newspaper by second class mail, a publisher MUST

    A. have met certain postal requirements and obtained a permit
    B. indicate whether he wants to use the single piece or the bulk rate
    C. make certain that the newspaper weighs less than one pound
    D. mark the newspaper *Second Class* on the top and bottom of the wrapper

20.____

21. Of the following types of information, the one which is NOT mentioned in the passage is the　　21.____

   A. class of mail to which parcel post belongs
   B. kinds of items which can be sent by each class of mail
   C. maximum weight for an item sent by fourth class mail
   D. postage rate for each of the four classes of mail

Questions 22-25.

DIRECTIONS: Questions 22 through 25 are to be answered SOLELY on the basis of the following paragraph.

A standard comprises characteristics attached to an aspect of a process or product by which it can be evaluated. Standardization is the development and adoption of standards. When they are formulated, standards are not usually the product of a single person, but represent the thoughts and ideas of a group, leavened with the knowledge and information which are currently available. Standards which do not meet certain basic requirements become a hindrance rather than an aid to progress. Standards must not only be correct, accurate, and precise in requiring no more and no less than what is needed for satisfactory results, but they must also be workable in the sense that their usefulness is not nullified by external conditions. Standards should also be acceptable to the people who use them. If they are not acceptable, they cannot be considered to be satisfactory, although they may possess all the other essential characteristics.

22. According to the above paragraph, a processing standard that requires the use of materials that cannot be procured is MOST likely to be　　22.____

   A. incomplete   B. unworkable
   C. inaccurate   D. unacceptable

23. According to the above paragraph, the construction of standards to which the performance of job duties should conform is MOST often　　23.____

   A. the work of the people responsible for seeing that the duties are properly performed
   B. accomplished by the person who is best informed about the functions involved
   C. the responsibility of the people who are to apply them
   D. attributable to the efforts of various informed persons

24. According to the above paragraph, when standards call for finer tolerances than those essential to the conduct of successful production operations, the effect of the standards on the improvement of production operations is　　24.____

   A. negative   B. negligible
   C. nullified   D. beneficial

25. The one of the following which is the MOST suitable title for the above paragraph is　　25.____

   A. THE EVALUATION OF FORMULATED STANDARDS
   B. THE ATTRIBUTES OF SATISFACTORY STANDARDS
   C. THE ADOPTION OF ACCEPTABLE STANDARDS
   D. THE USE OF PROCESS OR PRODUCT STANDARDS

KEY (CORRECT ANSWERS)

1. B	11. D
2. A	12. C
3. E	13. B
4. D	14. A
5. E	15. C
6. C	16. B
7. A	17. C
8. D	18. C
9. A	19. B
10. C	20. A

21. D
22. C
23. D
24. A
25. B

CLERICAL ABILITIES TEST

Clerical aptitude involves the ability to perceive pertinent detail in verbal or tabular material, to observe differences in copy, to proofread words and numbers, and to avoid perceptual errors in arithmetic computation.

NATURE OF THE TEST

Four types of clerical aptitude questions are presented in the Clerical Abilities Test. There are 120 questions with a short time limit. The test contains 30 questions on name and number checking, 30 on the arrangement of names in correct alphabetical order, 30 on simple arithmetic, and 30 on inspecting groups of letters and numbers. The questions have been arranged in groups or cycles of five questions of each type. The Clerical Abilities Test is primarily a test of speed in carrying out relatively simple clerical tasks. While accuracy on these tasks is important and will be taken into account in the scoring, experience has shown that many persons are so concerned about accuracy that they do the test more slowly than they should. Competitors should be cautioned that speed as well as accuracy is important to achieve a good score.

HOW THE TEST IS ADMINISTERED

Each competitor should be given a copy of the test booklet with sample questions on the cover page, an answer sheet, and a medium No. 2 pencil. Ten minutes are allowed to study the directions and sample questions and to answer the questions in the proper boxes on the two pages.
The separate answer sheet should be used for the test proper. Fifteen minutes are allowed for the test.

HOW THE TEST IS SCORED

The correct answers should be counted and recorded. The number of incorrect answers must also be counted because one-fourth of the number of incorrect answers is subtracted from the number of right answers. An omission is considered as neither a right nor a wrong answer. The score on this test is the number of right answers minus one-fourth of the number of wrong answers (fractions of one-half or less are dropped). For example, if an applicant had answered 89 questions correctly and 10 questions incorrectly, and had omitted 1 question, his score would be 87.

EXAMINATION SECTION

DIRECTIONS: This test contains four kinds of questions. There are some of each kind on each page in the booklet. The time limit for the test will be announced by the examiner.
Use the special pencil furnished by the examiner in marking your answers on the separate answer sheet. For each question, there are five suggested answers. Decide which answer is correct, find the number of the question on the answer sheet, and make a solid black mark between the dotted lines just below the letter of your answer. If you wish to change your answer, erase the first mark completely, do not merely cross it out.

SAMPLE QUESTIONS

In each line across the page there are three names or numbers that are much alike. Compare the three names or numbers and decide which ones are exactly alike. On the Sample Answer Sheet at the right, mark the answer
- A. if ALL THREE names or numbers are exactly ALIKE
- B. if only the FIRST and SECOND names or numbers are exactly ALIKE
- C. if only the FIRST and THIRD names or numbers are exactly ALIKE
- D. if only the SECOND and THIRD names or numbers are exactly ALIKE
- E. if ALL THREE names or numbers are DIFFERENT

I.	Davis Hazen	David Hozen	David Hazen
II.	Lois Appel	Lois Appel	Lois Apfel
III.	June Allan	Jane Allan	Jane Allan
IV.	10235	10235	10235
V.	32614	32164	32614

It will be to your advantage to learn what A, B, C, D, and E stand for. If you finish the sample questions before you are told to turn to the test, study them.

In the next group of sample questions, there is a name in a box at the left, and four other names in alphabetical order at the right. Find the correct space for the boxed name so that it will be in alphabetical order with the others, and mark the letter of that space as your answer.

VI. Jones, Jane

A. →
   Goodyear, G.L.
B. →
   Haddon, Harry
C. →
   Jackson, Mary
D. →
   Jenkins, William
E. →

VII. Kessler, Neilson

A. →
   Kessel, Carl
B. →
   Kessinger, D.J.
C. →
   Kessler, Karl
D. →
   Kessner, Lewis
E. →

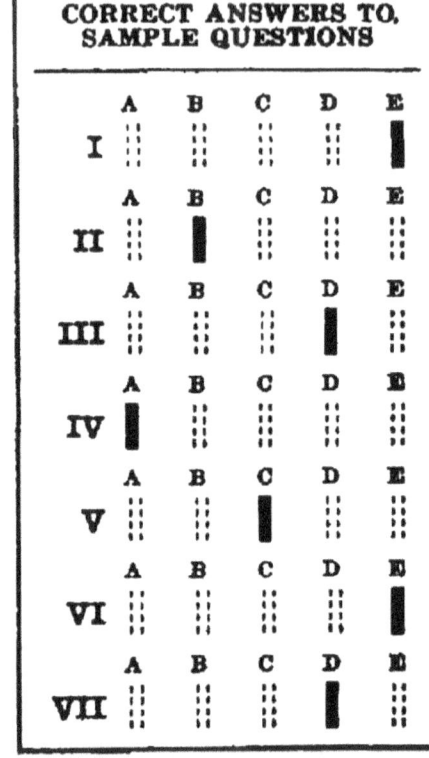

DIRECTIONS: In the following questions, complete the equation and find your answer among the list of suggested answers. Mark the Sample Answer Sheet A, B, C, or D for the answer you obtained; or if your answer is not among these, mark E for that question.

VIII. Add: 22
         +33

   A. 44   B. 45   C. 54   D. 55   E. None of these

IX. Subtract: 24
            - 3

   A. 20   B. 21   C. 27   D. 29   E. None of these

X. Multiply: 25
          x 5

   A. 100   B. 115   C. 125   D. 135   E. None of these

XI. Divide: 6/126̄

    A. 20   B. 22   C. 24   D. 26   E. None of these

DIRECTIONS: There is one set of suggested answers for the next group of sample questions. Do not try to memorize these answers, because there will be a different set on each age in the test.

To find the answer to a question, find which suggested answer contains numbers and letters, all of which appear in the question. If no suggested answer fits, mark E for that question.

XII. 8 N K 9 G T 4 6

XIII. T 9 7 Z 6 L 3 K

XIV. Z 7 G K 3 9 8 N

XV. 3 K 9 4 6 G Z L

XVI. Z N 7 3 8 K T 9

Suggested Answers
A = 7, 9, G, K
B = 8, 9, T, Z
C = 6, 7, K, Z
D = 6, 8, G, T
E = None of the above

After you have marked your answers to all the questions on the Sample Answer Sheets on this page and on the front page of the booklet, check them with the answers in the boxes marked Correct Answers To Sample Questions.

Questions 1-5.

In Questions 1 through 5, compare the three names or numbers, and mark
    A. if ALL THREE names or numbers are exactly ALIKE
    B. if only the FIRST and SECOND names or numbers are exactly ALIKE
    C. if only the FIRST and THIRD names or numbers are exactly ALIKE
    D. if only the SECOND and THIRD names or numbers are exactly ALIKE
    E. if ALL THREE names or numbers are DIFFERENT

1.   5261383   5261383   5261338

2.   8125690   8126690   8125609

3.   W.E. Johnston   W.E. Johnson   W.E. Johnson

4.   Vergil L. Muller   Vergil L. Muller   Vergil L. Muller

5. Atherton R. Warde   Asheton R. Warde   Atherton P. Warde

Questions 6-10.

In Questions 6 through 10, find the correct place for the name in the box

6. | Hackett, Gerald |

A. →
Habert, James
B. →
Hachett, J.J.
C. →
Hachetts, K. Larson
D. →
Hachettson, Leroy
E. →

7. | Margenroth, Alvin |

A. →
Margeroth, Albert
B. →
Margestein, Dan
C. →
Margestein, David
D. →
Margue, Edgar
E. →

8. | Bobbitt, Olivier E. |

A. →
Bobbitt, D. Olivier
B. →
Bobbitt, Olivia B
C. →
Bobbitt, Olivia H.
D. →
Bobbitt, R. Olivia
E. →

9. | Mosley, Werner |

A. →
Mosely, Albert J.
B. →
Mosley, Alvin
C. →
Mosley, S.M.
D. →
Mozley, Vinson N.
E. →

10. Youmuns, Frank L.

A. →
Youmons, Frank G.
B. →
Youmons, Frank H.
C. →
Youmons, Frank K.
D. →
Youmons, Frank M.
E. →

Questions 11-15.

11. Add: 43
         +32

   A. 55   B. 65   C. 66   D. 75   E. None of these

12. Subtract: 83
              - 4

   A. 73   B. 79   C. 80   D. 89   E. None of these

13. Multiply: 41
              x 7

   A. 281   B. 287   C. 291   D. 297   E. None of these

14. Divide: 6/306

   A. 44   B. 51   C. 52   D. 60   E. None of these

15. Add: 37
         +15

   A. 42   B. 52   C. 53   D. 62   E. None of these

Questions 16-20.

In Questions 16 through 20, find which one of the suggested answers appears in that question.

16.   6 2 5 K 4 P T G

17.   L 4 7 2 T 6 V K

18.   3 5 4 L 9 V T G

19.   G 4 K 7 L 3 5 Z

SUGGESTED ANSWERS
A = 4, 5, K, T
B = 4, 7, G, K
C = 2, 5, G, L
D = 2, 7, L, T
E = None of the above

20. 4 K 2 9 N 5 T G

Questions 21-25.

In Questions 21 through 25, compare the three names or numbers, and mark
    A. if ALL THREE names or numbers are exactly ALIKE
    B. if only the FIRST and SECOND names or numbers are exactly ALIKE
    C. if only the FIRST and THIRD names or numbers are exactly ALIKE
    D. if only the SECOND and THIRD names or numbers are exactly ALIKE
    E. if ALL THREE names or numbers are DIFFERENT

21. 2395890   2395890   2395890

22. 1926341   1926347   1926314

23. E. Owens McVey   E. Owen McVey   E. Owen McVay

24. Emily Neal Rouse   Emily Neal Rowse   Emily Neal Rowse

25. H. Merritt Audubon   H. Merriott Audubon H. Merritt Audubon

Questions 26-30.

In Questions 26 through 30, find the correct place for the name in the box.

26. | Watters, N.O. |

    A. →
        Waters, Charles L.
    B. →
        Waterson, Nina P.
    C. →
        Watson, Nora J.
    D. →
        Wattwood, Paul A.
    E. →

27. | Johnston, Edward |

    A. →
        Johnston, Edgar R.
    B. →
        Johnston, Edmond
    C. →
        Johnston, Edmund
    D. →
        Johnstone, Edmund A.
    E. →

28. Rensch, Adeline
    A. → Ramsay, Amos
    B. → Remschel, Augusta
    C. → Renshaw, Austin
    D. → Rentzel, Becky
    E. →

29. Schnyder, Maurice
    A. → Schneider, Martin
    B. → Schneider, Mertens
    C. → Schnyder, Newman
    D. → Schreibner, Norman
    E. →

30. Freedenburg, C. Erma
    A. → Freedenberg, Emerson
    B. → Freedenberg, Erma
    C. → Freedenberg, Erma E.
    D. → Freedinberg, Erma F.
    E. →

Questions 31-35.

31. Subtract: 68
             - 47

    A. 10   B. 11   C. 20   D. 22   E. None of these

32. Multiply: 50
             x 8

    A. 400   B. 408   C. 450   D. 458   E. None of these

33. Divide: 9/180

    A. 20   B. 29   C. 30   D. 39   E. None of these

34. Add: 78
        + 63

    A. 131   B. 140   C. 141   D. 151   E. None of these

35. Add: 89
    -70

    A. 9   B. 18   C. 19   D. 29   E. None of these

Questions 36-40.

In Questions 36 through 40, find which one of the suggested answers appears in that question.

36. 9 G Z 3 L 4 6 N

37. L 5 N K 4 3 9 V

38. 8 2 V P 9 L Z 5

39. V P 9 Z 5 L 8 7

40. 5 T 8 N 2 9 V L

SUGGESTED ANSWERS
A = 4, 9, L, V
B = 4, 5, N, Z
C = 5, 8, L, Z
D = 8, 9, N, V
E = None of the above

Questions 41-45.

In Questions 41 through 45, compare the three names or numbers, and mark
    A. if ALL THREE names or numbers are exactly ALIKE
    B. if only the FIRST and SECOND names or numbers are exactly ALIKE
    C. if only the FIRST and THIRD names or numbers are exactly ALIKE
    D. if only the SECOND and THIRD names or numbers are exactly ALIKE
    E. if ALL THREE names or numbers are DIFFERENT

41.	6219354	621354	6219354
42.	2312793	2312793	2312793
43.	1065407	1065407	1065047
44.	Francis Ransdell	Frances Ramsdell	Francis Ramsdell
45.	Cornelius Detwiler	Cornelius Detwiler	Cornelius Detwiler

Questions 46-50.

In Questions 46 through 50, find the correct place for the name in the box.

46. DeMattia, Jessica

A. →
DeLong, Jesse
B. →
DeMatteo, Jessie
C. →
Derby, Jessie S.
D. →
DeShazo, L.M.
E. →

47. Theriault, Louis

A. →
Therien, Annette
B. →
Therien, Elaine
C. →
Thibeault, Gerald
D. →
Thiebeault, Pierre
E. →

48. Gaston, M. Hubert

A. →
Gaston, Dorothy M.
B. →
Gaston, Henry N.
C. →
Gaston, Isabel
D. →
Gaston, M. Melvin
E. →

49. SanMiguel, Carlos

A. →
SanLuis, Juana
B. →
Santilli, Laura
C. →
Stinnett, Nellie
D. →
Stoddard, Victor
E. →

50. | DeLaTour, Hall F. |

A. →
DeLargy, Harold
B. →
DeLathouder, Hilda
C. →
Lathrop, Hillary
D. →
LaTour, Hulbert E.
E. →

Questions 51-55.

51. Multiply: 62
    x 5

    A. 300   B. 310   C. 315   D. 360   E. None of these

52. Divide: 3/153

    A. 41   B. 43   C. 51   D. 53   E. None of these

53. Add: 47
    +21

    A. 58   B. 59   C. 67   D. 68   E. None of these

54. Subtract: 87
    - 42

    A. 34   B. 35   C. 44   D. 45   E. None of these

55. Multiply: 37
    x 3

    A. 91   B. 101   C. 104   D. 114   E. None of these

Questions 56-60.

For Questions 56 through 60, find which one of the suggested answers appears in that question.

56. N 5 4 7 T K 3 Z

57. 8 5 3 V L 2 Z N

58. 7 2 5 N 9 K L V

59. 9 8 L 2 5 Z K V

60. Z 6 5 V 9 3 P N

SUGGESTED ANSWERS
A = 3, 8, K, N
B = 5, 8, N, V
C = 3, 9, V, Z
D = 5, 9, K, Z
E = None of the above

Questions 61-65.

In Questions 61 through 65, compare the three names or numbers, and mark
- A. if ALL THREE names or numbers are exactly ALIKE
- B. if only the FIRST and SECOND names or numbers are exactly ALIKE
- C. if only the FIRST and THIRD names or numbers are exactly ALIKE
- D. if only the SECOND and THIRD names or numbers are exactly ALIKE
- E. if ALL THREE names or numbers are DIFFERENT

61.	6452054	6452654	6452054
62.	8501268	8501268	8501286
63	Ella Burk Newham	Ella Burk Newnham	Elena Burk Newnham
64.	Jno. K. Ravencroft	Jno. H. Ravencroft	Jno. H. Ravencoft
65.	Martin Wills Pullen	Martin Wills Pulen	Martin Wills Pullen

Questions 66-70.

In Questions 66 through 70, find the correct place for the name in the box.

66. O'Bannon, M.J.
- A. →
  O'Beirne, B.B.
- B. →
  Oberlin, E.L.
- C. →
  Oberneir, L.P.
- D. →
  O'Brian, S.F.
- E. →

67. Entsminger, Jacob
- A. →
  Ensminger, J.
- B. →
  Entsminger, J.A.
- C. →
  Entsminger, Jack
- D. →
  Entsminger, James
- E. →

68. Iacone, Pete R.

A. →
Iacone, Pedro
B. →
Iacone, Pedro M.
C. →
Iacone, Peter F.
D. →
Iascone, Peter W.
E. →

69. Sheppard, Gladys

A. →
Shepard, Dwight
B. →
Shepard, F.H.
C. →
Shephard, Louise
D. →
Shepperd, Stella
E. →

70. Thackton, Melvin T.

A. →
Thackston, Milton G.
B. →
Thackston, Milton W.
C. →
Thackston, Theodore
D. →
Thackston, Thomas G.
E. →

Questions 71-75.

71. Divide: $7\overline{)357}$

   A. 51   B. 52   C. 53   D. 54   E. None of these

72. Add: 58
         +27

   A. 75   B. 84   C. 85   D. 95   E. None of these

73. Subtract: 86
              - 57

   A. 18   B. 29   C. 38   D. 39   E. None of these

74. Multiply: 68
    x 4

    A. 242   B. 264   C. 272   D. 274   E. None of these

75. Divide: 9/639

    A. 71   B. 73   C. 81   D. 83   E. None of these

Questions 76-80.

For Questions 76 through 80, find which one of the suggested answers appears in that question.

76. 6 Z T N 8 7 4 V

77. V 7 8 6 N 5 P L

78. N 7 P V 8 4 2 L

79. 7 8 G 4 3 V L T

80. 4 8 G 2 T N 6 L

SUGGESTED ANSWERS
A = 2, 7, L, N
B = 2, 8, T, V
C = 6, 8, L, T
D = 6, 7, N, V
E = None of the above

Questions 81-85.

In Questions 81 through 85, compare the three names or numbers, and mark
  A. if ALL THREE names or numbers are exactly ALIKE
  B. if only the FIRST and SECOND names or numbers are exactly ALIKE
  C. if only the FIRST and THIRD names or numbers are exactly ALIKE
  D. if only the SECOND and THIRD names or numbers are exactly ALIKE
  E. if ALL THREE names or numbers are DIFFERENT

81. 3457988	3457986	3457986
82. 4695682	4695862	4695682
83. Stricklund Kanedy	Stricklund Kanedy	Stricklund Kanedy
84. Joy Harbor Witner	Joy Harloe Witner	Joy Harloe Witner
85. R.M.O. Uberroth	R.M.O. Uberroth	R.N.O. Uberroth

Questions 86-90.

In Questions 86 through 90, find the correct place for the name in the box.

86. Dunlavey, M. Hilary

A. →
Dunleavy, Hilary G.
B. →
Dunleavy, Hilary K.
C. →
Dunleavy, Hilary S.
D. →
Dunleavy, Hilery W.
E. →

87. Yarbrough, Maria

A. →
Yabroudy, Margy
B. →
Yarboro, Marie
C. →
Yarborough, Marina
D. →
Yarborough, Mary
E. →

88. Prouty, Martha

A. →
Proutey, Margaret
B. →
Proutey, Maude
C. →
Prouty, Myra
D. →
Prouty, Naomi
E. →

89. Pawlowicz, Ruth M.

A. →
Pawalek, Edward
B. →
Pawelek, Flora G.
C. →
Pawlowski, Joan M.
D. →
Pawtowski, Wanda
E. →

90. Vanstory, George

A. →
   Vanover, Eva
B. →
   VanSwinderen, Floyd
C. →
   VanSyckle, Harry
D. →
   Vanture, Laurence
E. →

Questions 91-95

91. Add: 28
          +35

    A. 53   B. 62   C. 64   D. 73   E. None of these

92. Subtract: 78
              -69

    A. 7   B. 8   C. 18   D. 19   E. None of these

93. Multiply: 86
              x 6

    A. 492   B. 506   C. 516   D. 526   E. None of these

94. Divide: 8/648

    A. 71   B. 76   C. 81   D. 89   E. None of these

95. Add: 97
          +34

    A. 131   B. 132   C. 140   D. 141   E. None of these

Questions 96-100.

For Questions 96 through 100, find which one of the suggested answers appears in that question.

96. V 5 7 Z N 9 4 T

97. 4 6 P T 2 N K 9

98. 6 4 N 2 P 8 Z K

99. 7 P 5 2 4 N K T

100. K T 8 5 4 N 2 P

SUGGESTED ANSWERS
A = 2, 5, N, Z
B = 4, 5, N, P
C = 2, 9, P, T
D = 4, 9, T, Z
E = None of the above

Questions 101-105.

In Questions 101 through 105, compare the three names or numbers, and mark
- A. if ALL THREE names or numbers are exactly ALIKE
- B. if only the FIRST and SECOND names or numbers are exactly ALIKE
- C. if only the FIRST and THIRD names or numbers are exactly ALIKE
- D. if only the SECOND and THIRD names or numbers are exactly ALIKE
- E. if ALL THREE names or numbers are DIFFERENT

101. 1592514	1592574	1592574
102. 2010202	2010202	2010220
103. 6177396	6177936	6177396
104. Drusilla S. Ridgeley	Drusilla S. Ridgeley	Drusilla S. Ridgeley
105. Andrei I. Toumantzev	Andrei I. Tourmantzev	Andrei I. Toumantzov

Questions 106-110.

In Questions 106 through 110, find the correct place for the name in the box.

106. | Fitzsimmons, Hugh |

- A. →
  Fitts, Harold
- B. →
  Fitzgerald, June
- C. →
  FitzGibbon, Junius
- D. →
  FitzSimons, Martin
- E. →

107. | D'Amato, Vincent |

- A. →
  Daly, Steven
- B. →
  D'Amboise, S. Vincent
- C. →
  Daniel, Vail
- D. →
  DeAlba, Valentina
- E. →

108. Schaeffer, Roger D.

A. → Schaffert, Evelyn M.
B. → Schaffner, Margaret M.
C. → Schafhirt, Milton G.
D. → Shafer, Richard E.
E. →

109. White-Lewis, Cecil

A. → Whitelaw, Cordelia
B. → White-Leigh, Nancy
C. → Whitely, Rodney
D. → Whitlock, Warren
E. →

110. VanDerHeggen, Don

A. → VanDemark, Doris
B. → Vandenberg, H.E.
C. → VanDercook, Marie
D. → vanderLinden, Robert
E. →

Questions 111-115.

111. Add: 75
     +49

   A. 124   B. 125   C. 134   D. 225   E. None of these

112. Subtract: 69
     - 45

   A. 14   B. 23   C. 24   D. 26   E. None of these

113. Multiply: 36
     x 8

   A. 246   B. 262   C. 288   D. 368   E. None of these

114. Divide: 8/328̄

    A. 31   B. 41   C. 42   D. 48   E. None of these

115. Multiply: 58
             x 9

    A. 472   B. 513   C. 521   D. 522   E. None of these

Questions 116-120.

For Questions 116 through 120, find which one of the suggested answers appears in that question.

116. Z 3 N P G 5 4 2

117. 6 N 2 8 G 4 P T

118. 6 N 4 T V G 8 2

119. T 3 P 4 N 8 G 2

120. 6 7 K G N 2 L 5

SUGGESTED ANSWERS:
A = 2, 3, G, N
B = 2, 6, N, T
C = 3, 4, G, K
D = 4, 6, K, T
E = None of the above

KEY (CORRECT ANSWERS)

1. B	21. A	41. A	61. C	81. D	101. D
2. E	22. E	42. A	62. B	82. C	102. B
3. D	23. E	43. B	63. E	83. A	103. C
4. A	24. D	44. E	64. E	84. D	104. A
5. E	25. C	45. A	65. C	85. B	105. E
6. E	26. D	46. C	66. A	86. A	106. D
7. A	27. D	47. A	667. D	87. E	107. B
8. D	28. C	48. D	68. C	88. C	108. A
9. B	29. C	49. B	69. D	89. C	109. C
10. E	30. D	50. C	70. E	90. B	110. D
11. D	31. E	51. B	71. A	91. E	111. A
12. B	32. A	52. C	72. C	92. E	112. C
13. B	33. A	53. D	73. B	93. C	113. C
14. B	34. C	54. D	74. C	94. C	114. B
15. B	35. C	55. E	75. A	95. A	115. D
16. A	36. E	56. E	76. D	96. D	116. A
17. D	37. A	57. B	77. D	97. C	117. B
18. E	38. C	58. E	78. A	98. E	118. B
19. B	39. C	59. D	79. E	99. B	119. A
20. A	40. D	60. C	80. C	100. B	120. E

NAME AND NUMBER COMPARISONS

COMMENTARY

This test seeks to measure your ability and disposition to do a job carefully and accurately, your attention to exactness and preciseness of detail, your alertness and versatility in discerning similarities and differences between things, and your power in systematically handling written language symbols.

It is actually a test of your ability to do academic and/or clerical work, using the basic elements of verbal (qualitative) and mathematical (quantitative) learning—words and numbers.

EXAMINATION SECTION

TEST 1

DIRECTIONS: In each line across the page there are three names or numbers that are much alike. Compare the three names or numbers and decide which ones are exactly alike. *PRINT IN THE SPACE AT THE RIGHT THE LETTER:*
  A. if all THREE names or numbers are exactly alike
  B. if only the FIRST and SECOND names or numbers are ALIKE
  C. if only the FIRST and THIRD names or numbers are alike
  D. if only the SECOND or THIRD names or numbers are alike
  E. if ALL THREE names or numbers are DIFFERENT

1.	Davis Hazen	David Hozen	David Hazen	1.____
2.	Lois Appel	Lois Appel	Lois Apfel	2.____
3.	June Allan	Jane Allan	Jane Allan	3.____
4.	10235	10235	10235	4.____
5.	32614	32164	32614	5.____

TEST 2

1.	2395890	2395890	2395890	1.____
2.	1926341	1926347	1926314	2.____
3.	E. Owens McVey	E. Owen McVey	E. Owen McVay	3.____
4.	Emily Neal Rouse	Emily Neal Rowse	Emily Neal Rowse	4.____
5.	H. Merritt Audubon	H. Merriott Audubon	H. Merritt Audubon	5.____

TEST 3

1.	6219354	6219354	6219354	1.____
2.	231793	2312793	2312793	2.____
3.	1065407	1065407	1065047	3.____
4.	Francis Ransdell	Frances Ramsdell	Francis Ramsdell	4.____
5.	Cornelius Detwiler	Cornelius Detwiler	Cornelius Detwiler	5.____

TEST 4

1.	6452054	6452564	6542054	1.____
2.	8501268	8501268	8501286	2.____
3.	Ella Burk Newham	Ella Burk Newnham	Elena Burk Newnham	3.____
4.	Jno. K. Ravencroft	Jno. H. Ravencroft	Jno. H. Ravencoft	4.____
5.	Martin Wills Pullen	Martin Wills Pulen	Martin Wills Pullen	5.____

TEST 5

1.	3457988	3457986	3457986	1.____
2.	4695682	4695862	4695682	2.____
3.	Stricklund Kaneydy	Sticklund Kanedy	Stricklund Kanedy	3.____
4.	Joy Harlor Witner	Joy Harloe Witner	Joy Harloe Witner	4.____
5.	R.M.O. Uberroth	R.M.O. Uberroth	R.N.O. Uberroth	5.____

3

TEST 6

1.	1592514	1592574	1592574	1.____
2.	2010202	2010202	2010220	2.____
3.	6177396	6177936	6177396	3.____
4.	Drusilla S. Ridgeley	Drusilla S. Ridgeley	Drusilla S. Ridgeley	4.____
5.	Andrei I. Tooumantzev	Andrei I. Tourmantzev	Andrei I. Toumantzov	5.____

TEST 7

1.	5261383	5261383	5261338	1.____
2.	8125690	8126690	8125609	2.____
3.	W.E. Johnston	W.E. Johnson	W.E. Johnson	3.____
4.	Vergil L. Muller	Vergil L. Muller	Vergil L. Muller	4.____
5.	Atherton R. Warde	Asheton R. Warde	Atherton P. Warde	5.____

TEST 8

1.	013469.5	023469.5	02346.95	1.____
2.	33376	333766	333766	2.____
3.	Ling-Temco-Vought	Ling-Tenco-Vought	Ling-Temco Vought	3.____
4.	Lorilard Corp.	Lorillard Corp.	Lorrilard Corp.	4.____
5.	American Agronomics Corporation	American Agronomics Corporation	American Agronomic Corporation	5.____

TEST 9

1.	436592864	436592864	436592864	1.____
2.	197765123	197755123	197755123	2.____
3.	Dewaay Cortvriendt International S.A.	Deway Cortvriendt International S.A.	Deway Corturiendt International S.A.	3.____
4.	Crédit Lyonnais	Crèdit Lyonnais	Crèdit Lyonais	4.____
5.	Algemene Bank Nederland N.V.	Algamene Bank Nederland N.V.	Algemene Bank Naderland N.V.	5.____

TEST 10

1.	00032572	0.0032572	00032522	1.____
2.	399745	399745	398745	2.____
3.	Banca Privata Finanziaria S.p.A.	Banca Privata Finanzaria S.P.A.	Banca Privata Finanziaria S.P.A.	3.____
4.	Eastman Dillon, Union Securities & Co.	Eastman Dillon, Union Securities Co.	Eastman Dillon, Union Securities & Co.	4.____
5.	Arnhold and S. Bleichroeder, Inc.	Arnhold & S. Bleichroeder, Inc.	Arnold and S. Bleichroeder, Inc.	5.____

TEST 11

DIRECTIONS: Answer the questions below on the basis of the following instructions: For each such numbered set of names, addresses, and numbers listed in Columns I and II, select your answer from the following options:
A. The names in Columns I and II are different
B. The addresses in Columns I and II are different
C. The numbers in Columns I and II are different
D. The names, addresses and numbers are identical

1. Francis Jones
   62 Stately Avenue
   96-12446

   Francis Jones
   62 Stately Avenue
   96-21446

   1.____

2. Julio Montez
   19 Ponderosa Road
   56-73161

   Julio Montez
   19 Ponderosa Road
   56-71361

   2.____

3. Mary Mitchell
   2314 Melbourne Drive
   68-92172

   Mary Mitchell
   2314 Melbourne Drive
   68-92172

   3.____

4. Harry Patterson
   25 Dunne Street
   14-33430

   Harry Patterson
   25 Dunne Street
   14-34330

   4.____

5. Patrick Murphy
   171 West Hosmer Street
   93-81214

   Patrick Murphy
   171 West Hosmer Street
   93-18214

   5.____

TEST 12

1. August Schultz
   816 St. Clair Avenue
   53-40149

   August Schultz
   816 St. Claire Avenue
   53-40149

   1._____

2. George Taft
   72 Runnymede Street
   47-04033

   George Taft
   72 Runnymede Street
   47-04023

   2._____

3. Angus Henderson
   1418 Madison Street
   81-76375

   Angus Henderson
   1418 Madison Street
   81-76375

   3._____

4. Carolyn Mazur
   12 Rivenlew Road
   38-99615

   Carolyn Mazur
   12 Rivervane Road
   38-99615

   4._____

5. Adele Russell
   1725 Lansing Lane
   72-91962

   Adela Russell
   1725 Lansing Lane
   72-91962

   5._____

TEST 13

DIRECTIONS: The following questions are based on the instructions given below. In each of the following questions, the 3-line name and address in Column I is the master-list entry, and the 3-line entry in Column II is the information to be checked against the master list.
If there is one line that is NOT exactly alike, mark your answer A.
If there are two lines NOT exactly alike, mark your answer B.
If there are three lines NOT exactly alike, mark your answer C.
If the lines ALL are exactly alike, mark your answer D.

1. Jerome A. Jackson
   1243 14th Avenue
   New York, N.Y. 10023

   Jerome A. Johnson
   1234 14th Avenue
   New York, N.Y. 10023

   1.____

2. Sophie Strachtheim
   33-28 Connecticut Ave.
   Far Rockaway, N.Y. 11697

   Sophie Strachtheim
   33-28 Connecticut Ave.
   Far Rockaway, N.Y. 11697

   2.____

3. Elisabeth NT. Gorrell
   256 Exchange St
   New York, N.Y. 10013

   Elizabeth NT. Correll
   256 Exchange St.
   New York, N.Y. 10013

   3.____

4. Maria J. Gonzalez
   7516 E. Sheepshead Rd.
   Brooklyn, N.Y. 11240

   Maria J. Gonzalez
   7516 N. Shepshead Rd.
   Brooklyn, N.Y. 11240

   4.____

5. Leslie B. Brautenweiler
   21-57A Seller Terr.
   Flushing, N.Y. 11367

   Leslie B. Brautenwieler
   21-75ASeiler Terr.
   Flushing, N.J. 11367

   5.____

KEY (CORRECT ANSWERS)

TEST 1	TEST 2	TEST 3	TEST 4	TEST 5	TEST 6	TEST 7
1. E	1. A	1. A	1. E	1. D	1. D	1. B
2. B	2. E	2. A	2. B	2. C	2. B	2. E
3. D	3. E	3. B	3. E	3. E	3. C	3. D
4. A	4. D	4. E	4. E	4. D	4. A	4. A
5. C	5. C	5. A	5. C	5. B	5. E	5. E

TEST 8	TEST 9	TEST 10	TEST 11	TEST 12	TEST 13
1. E	1. A	1. E	1. C	1. B	1. B
2. D	2. D	2. B	2. C	2. C	2. D
3. E	3. E	3. E	3. D	3. D	3. A
4. E	4. E	4. C	4. C	4. B	4. A
5. B	5. E	5. E	5. C	5. A	5. C

NAME AND NUMBER CHECKING
EXAMINATION SECTION
TEST 1

DIRECTIONS: This test is designed to measure your speed/and accuracy. You are urged to work both quickly and accurately and to do correctly as many lists as you can in the time allowed. The test consists of lists or pairs of names and numbers. Count the number of IDENTICAL pairs in each list. Then, select the correct number, 1, 2, 3, 4, 5, and indicate your choice in the space at the right. Two sample questions are presented for your guidance, together with the correct solutions.

SAMPLE LIST A
Adelphi College – Adelphia College
Braxton Corp – Braxeton Corp.
Wassaic State School – Wassaic State School
Central Islip State Hospital – Central Isllip State Hospital
Greenwich House – Greenwich House

NOTE: There are only two correct pairs—Wassaic State School and Greenwich House. Therefore, the CORRECT answer is 2.

SAMPLE LIST B
78453694 – 78453684
784530 – 784530
533 – 534
67845 – 67845
2368745 – 2368755

NOTE: There are only two correct pairs—784530 and 67845. Therefore, the CORRECT answer is 2.

LIST 1   1.____
    Diagnostic Clinic   – Diagnostic Clinic
    Yorkville Health   – Yorkville Health
    Meinhard Clinic   – Meinhart Clinic
    Corlears Clinic   – Carlears Clinic
    Tremont Diagnostic – Tremont Diagnostic

LIST 2   2.____
    73526   – 73526
    7283627198   – 7283627198
    627   – 637
    728352617283 – 7283526178282
    6281   – 6281

2 (#1)

LIST 3   3.____
    Jefferson Clinic — Jeffersen Clinic
    Mott Haven Center — Mott Havan Center
    Bronx Hospital — Bronx Hospital
    Montefiore Hospital — Montifeore Hospital
    Beth Isreal Hospital — Beth Israel Hospital

LIST 4   4.____
    936271826 — 936371826
    5271 — 5291
    82637192037 — 82637192037
    527182 — 5271882
    726354256 - 72635456

LIST 5   5.____
    Trinity Hospital — Trinity Hospital
    Central Harlem — Centrel Harlem
    St. Luke's Hospital — St. Lukes' Hospital
    Mt. Sinai Hospital — Mt. Sinia Hospital
    N.Y. Dispensery — N.Y. Dispensary

LIST 6   6.____
    725361552637 — 725361555637
    7526378 — 7526377
    6975 — 6975
    82637481028 — 82637481028
    3427 — 3429

LIST 7   7.____
    Misericordia Hospital — Miseracordia Hospital
    Lebonan Hospital — Lebanon Hospital
    Gouverneur Hospital — Gouverner Hospital
    German Polyclinic — German Policlinic
    French Hospital — French Hospital

LIST 8   8.____
    8277364933251 — 827364933351
    63728 — 63728
    367281 — 367281
    62733846273 — 6273846293
    62836 - 6283

LIST 9   9.____
    King's County Hospital — Kings County Hospital
    St. Johns Long Island — St. John's Long Island
    Bellevue Hospital — Bellvue Hospital
    Beth David Hospital — Beth David Hospital
    Samaritan Hospital — Samariton Hospital

LIST 10
 62836454   – 62836455
 42738267   – 42738369
 573829   – 573829
 738291627874   – 738291627874
 725   - 735

10.____

LIST 11
 Bloomingdal Clinic   – Bloomingdale Clinic
 Communitty Hospital   – Community Hospital
 Metroplitan Hospital   – Metropoliton Hospital
 Lenox Hill Hospital   – Lonex Hill Hospital
 Lincoln Hospital   – Lincoln Hospital

11.____

LIST 12
 6283364728   – 6283648
 627385   – 627383
 54283902   – 54283602
 63354   – 63354
 7283562781   - 7283562781

12.____

LIST 13
 Sydenham Hospital   – Sydanham Hospital
 Roosevalt Hospital   – Roosevelt Hospital
 Vanderbilt Clinic   – Vanderbild Clinic
 Women's Hospital   – Woman's Hospital
 Flushing Hospital   – Flushing Hospital

13.____

LIST 14
 62738   – 62738
 727355542321   – 72735542321
 263849332   – 263849332
 262837   – 263837
 47382912   - 47382922

14.____

LIST 15
 Episcopal Hospital   – Episcapal Hospital
 Flower Hospital   – Flouer Hospital
 Stuyvesent Clinic   – Stuyvesant Clinic
 Jamaica Clinic   – Jamaica Clinic
 Ridgwood Clinic   – Ridgewood Clinic

15.____

LIST 16
 628367299   – 628367399
 111   – 111
 118293304829   – 1182839489
 4448   – 4448
 333693678   - 333693678

16.____

4 (#1)

LIST 17   17.____
    Arietta Crane Farm   – Areitta Crane Farm
    Bikur Chilim Home   – Bikur Chilom Home
    Burke Foundation   – Burke Foundation
    Blythedale Home   – Blythdale Home
    Campbell Cottages   – Cambell Cottages

LIST 18   18.____
    32123   – 32132
    273893326783   – 27389326783
    473829   – 473829
    7382937   – 7383937
    3628890122332   - 36289012332

LIST 19   19.____
    Caraline Rest   – Caroline Rest
    Loreto Rest   – Loretto Rest
    Edgewater Creche   – Edgwater Creche
    Holiday Farm   – Holiday Farm
    House of St. Giles   – House of st. Giles

LIST 20   20.____
    557286777   – 55728677
    3678902   – 3678892
    1567839   – 1567839
    7865434712   – 7865344712
    9927382   - 9927382

LIST 21   21.____
    Isabella Home   – Isabela Home
    James A. Moore Home   – James A. More Home
    The Robin's Nest   – The Roben's Nest
    Pelham Home   – Pelam Home
    St. Eleanora's Home   – St. Eleanora's Home

LIST 22   22.____
    273648293048   – 273648293048
    334   – 334
    7362536478   – 7362536478
    7362819273   – 7362819273
    7362   - 7363

LIST 23   23.____
    St. Pheobe's Mission   – St. Phebe's Mission
    Seaside Home   – Seaside Home
    Speedwell Society   – Speedwell Society
    Valeria Home   – Valera Home
    Wiltwyck   - Wildwyck

LIST 24
- 63728 – 63738
- 63728192736 – 63728192738
- 428 – 458
- 62738291527 – 62738291529
- 63728192 - 63728192

24.____

LIST 25
- McGaffin – McGafin
- David Ardslee – David Ardslee
- Axton Supply – Axeton Supply Co
- Alice Russell – Alice Russell
- Dobson Mfg. Co. – Dobsen Mfg. Co.

25.____

KEY (CORRECT ANSWERS)

1.	3	11.	1
2.	3	12.	2
3.	1	13.	1
4.	1	14.	2
5.	1	15.	1
6.	2	16.	3
7.	1	17.	1
8.	2	18.	1
9.	1	19.	1
10.	2	20.	2

21.	1
22.	4
23.	2
24.	1
25.	2

TEST 2

DIRECTIONS: This test is designed to measure your speed/and accuracy. You are urged to work both quickly and accurately and to do correctly as many lists as you can in the time allowed. The test consists of lists or pairs of names and numbers. Count the number of IDENTICAL pairs in each list. Then, select the correct number, 1, 2, 3, 4, 5, and indicate your choice in the space at the right.

LIST 1
    82637381028   – 82637281028
    928   – 928
    72937281028   – 72937281028
    7362   – 7362
    927382615   – 927382615

1.____

LIST 2
    Albee Theatre   – Albee Theatre
    Lapland Lumber Co.   – Laplund Lumber Co.
    Adelphi College   – Adelphi College
    Jones & Son Inc.   – Jones & Sons Inc.
    S.W. Ponds Co.   – S.W. Ponds Co.

2.____

LIST 3
    85345   – 85345
    895643278   – 895643277
    726352   – 726353
    632685   – 632685
    7263524   – 7236524

3.____

LIST 4
    Eagle Library   – Eagle Library
    Dodge Ltd.   – Dodge Co.
    Stromberg Carlson   – Stromberg Carlsen
    Clairice Ling   – Clairice Linng
    Mason Book Co.   – Matson Book Co.

4.____

LIST 5
    66273   – 66273
    629   – 629
    7382517283   – 7382517283
    637281   – 639281
    2738261   – 2788261

5.____

LIST 6
    Robert MacColl   – Robert McColl
    Buick Motor   – Buck Motors
    Murray Bay & Co. Ltd.   – Murray Bay Co. Ltd.
    L.T. Ltyle   – L.T. Lyttle
    A.S. Landas   – A.S. Landas

6.____

LIST 7　　　　　　　　　　　　　　　　　　　　　　　　　　　　　　7.____
    6271526374890　　　− 627152637490
    73526189　　　　　− 73526189
    5372　　　　　　　　− 5392
    637281142　　　　　− 63728124
    4783946　　　　　　− 4783046

LIST 8　　　　　　　　　　　　　　　　　　　　　　　　　　　　　　8.____
    Tyndall Burke　　　　　− Tyndell Burke
    W. Briehl　　　　　　　− W. Briehl
    Burritt Publishing Co.　− Buritt Publishing Co.
    Frederick Breyer & Co.　− Frederick Breyer Co.
    Bailey Buulard　　　　 − Bailey Bullard

LIST 9　　　　　　　　　　　　　　　　　　　　　　　　　　　　　　9.____
    634　　　　　　　　　− 634
    16837　　　　　　　　− 163837
    273892223678　　　　− 27389223678
    527182　　　　　　　− 527782
    3628901223　　　　　− 3629002223

LIST 10　　　　　　　　　　　　　　　　　　　　　　　　　　　　　10.____
    Ernest Boas　　　　　− Ernest Boas
    Rankin Barne　　　　　− Rankin Barnes
    Edward Appley　　　　− Edward Appely
    Camel　　　　　　　　− Camel
    Caiger Food Co.　　　− Caiger Food Co.

LIST 11　　　　　　　　　　　　　　　　　　　　　　　　　　　　　11.____
    6273　　　　　　　　　− 6273
    322　　　　　　　　　− 332
    15672839　　　　　　− 15672839
    63728192637　　　　　− 63728192639
    738　　　　　　　　　− 738

LIST 12　　　　　　　　　　　　　　　　　　　　　　　　　　　　　12.____
    Wells Fargo Co.　　　　− Wells Fargo Co.
    W.D. Brett　　　　　　− W.D. Britt
    Tassco Co.　　　　　　− Tassko Co.
    Republic Mills　　　　　− Republic Mill
    R.W. Burnham　　　　　− R.W. Burhnam

LIST 13　　　　　　　　　　　　　　　　　　　　　　　　　　　　　13.____
    7253529152　　　　　− 7283529152
    6283　　　　　　　　　− 6383
    52839102738　　　　　− 5283910238
    308　　　　　　　　　− 398
    82637201927　　　　　− 8263720127

LIST 14
- Schumacker Co. — Shumacker Co.
- C.H. Caiger — C.H. Caiger
- Abraham Strauss — Abram Straus
- B.F. Boettjer — B.F. Boettijer
- Cut-Rate Store — Cut-Rate Stores

14.____

LIST 15
- 15273826 — 15273826
- 72537 — 73537
- 726391027384 — 62639107384
- 637389 — 627399
- 725382910 — 725382910

15.____

LIST 16
- Hixby Ltd. — Hixby Lt'd.
- S. Reiner — S. Riener
- Reynard Co. — Reynord Co.
- Esso Gassoline Co. — Esso Gasolene Co.
- Belle Brock — Belle Brock

16.____

LIST 17
- 7245 — 7245
- 819263728192 — 819263728172
- 682537289 — 682537298
- 789 — 789
- 82936542891 — 82936542891

17.____

LIST 18
- Joseph Cartwright — Joseph Cartwrite
- Foote Food Co. — Foot Food Co.
- Weiman & Held — Weiman & Held
- Sanderson Shoe Co. — Sandersen Shoe Co.
- A.M. Byrne — A.N. Byrne

18.____

LIST 19
- 4738267 — 4738277
- 63728 — 63729
- 6283628901 — 6283628991
- 918264 — 918264
- 263728192037 — 2637728192073

19.____

LIST 20
- Exray Laboratories — Exray Labratories
- Curley Toy Co. — Curly Toy Co.
- J. Lauer & Cross — J. Laeur & Cross
- Mireco Brands — Mireco Brands
- Sandor Lorand — Sandor Larand

20.____

4 (#2)

LIST 21   21.____
   607   – 609
   6405   – 6403
   976   – 996
   101267   – 101267
   2065432   – 20965432

LIST 22   22.____
   John Macy & Sons   – John Macy & Son
   Venus Pencil Co.   – Venus Pencil Co.
   Nell McGinnis   – Nell McGinnis
   McCutcheon & Co.   – McCutcheon & Co.
   Sun-Tan Oil   – Sun-Tan Oil

LIST 23   23.____
   703345700   – 703345700
   46754   – 466754
   3367490   – 3367490
   3379   – 3778
   47384   – 47394

LIST 24   24.____
   arthritis   – arthritis
   asthma   – asthma
   endocrine   – endocrene
   gastro-enterological – gastrol-enteralogical
   orthopedic   – orthopedic

LIST 25   25.____
   743829432   – 743828432
   998   – 998
   732816253902 – 732816252902
   46829   – 46830
   7439120249   – 7439210249

KEY (CORRECT ANSWERS)

1.	4	11.	3
2.	3	12.	1
3.	2	13.	1
4.	1	14.	1
5.	2	15.	2
6.	1	16.	1
7.	2	17.	3
8.	1	18.	1
9.	1	19.	1
10.	3	20.	1

21.	1
22.	4
23.	2
24.	3
25.	1

RECORD KEEPING
EXAMINATION SECTION
TEST 1

DIRECTIONS: Each question or incomplete statement is followed by several suggested answers or completions. Select the one that BEST answers the question or completes the statement. *PRINT THE LETTER OF THE CORRECT ANSWER IN THE SPACE AT THE RIGHT.*

Questions 1-15.

DIRECTIONS: Questions 1 through 15 are to be answered on the basis of the following list of company names below. Arrange a file alphabetically, word-by-word, disregarding punctuation, conjunctions, and apostrophes. Then answer the questions.

    A Bee C Reading Materials
    ABCO Parts
    A Better Course for Test Preparation
    AAA Auto Parts Co.
    A-Z Auto Parts, Inc.
    Aabar Books
    Abbey, Joanne
    Boman-Sylvan Law Firm
    BMW Autowerks
    C Q Service Company
    Chappell-Murray, Inc.
    E&E Life Insurance
    Emcrisco
    Gigi Arts
    Gordon, Jon & Associates
    SOS Plumbing
    Schmidt, J.B. Co.

1. Which of these files should appear FIRST?   1.____
   A. ABCO Parts
   B. A Bee C Reading Materials
   C. A Better Course for Test Preparation
   D. AAA Auto Parts Co.

2. Which of these files should appear SECOND?   2.____
   A. A-Z Auto Parts, Inc.
   B. A Bee C Reading Materials
   C. A Better Course for Test Preparation
   D. AAA Auto Parts Co.

3. Which of these files should appear THIRD?
   A. ABCO Parts
   B. A Bee C Reading Materials
   C. Aabar Books
   D. AAA Auto Parts Co.

   3.____

4. Which of these files should appear FOURTH?
   A. Aabar Books
   B. ABCO Parts
   C. Abbey, Joanne
   D. AAA Auto Parts Co.

   4.____

5. Which of these files should appear LAST?
   A. Gordon, Jon & Associates
   B. Gigi Arts
   C. Schmidt, J.B. Co.
   D. SOS Plumbing

   5.____

6. Which of these files should appear between A-Z Auto Parts, Inc. and Abbey, Joanne?
   A. A Bee C Reading Materials
   B. AAA Auto Parts Co.
   C. ABCO Parts
   D. A Better Course for Test Preparation

   6.____

7. Which of these files should appear between ABCO Parts and Aabar Books?
   A. A Bee C Reading Materials
   B. Abbey, Joanne
   C. Aabar Books
   D. A-Z Auto Parts

   7.____

8. Which of these files should appear between Abbey, Joanne and Boman-Sylvan Law Firm?
   A. A Better Course for Test Preparation
   B. BMW Autowerks
   C. Chappell-Murray, Inc.
   D. Aabar Books

   8.____

9. Which of these files should appear between Abbey, Joanne and C Q Service?
   A. A-Z Auto Parts, Inc.
   B. BMW Autowerks
   C. Choices A and B
   D. Chappell-Murray, Inc.

   9.____

10. Which of these files should appear between C Q Service Company and Emcrisco?
    A. Chappell-Murray, Inc.
    B. E&E Life Insurance
    C. Gigi Arts
    D. Choices A and B

    10.____

11. Which of these files should NOT appear between C Q Service Company and E&E Life Insurance?
    A. Gordon, Jon & Associates
    B. Emcrisco
    C. Gigi Arts
    D. All of the above

    11.____

12. Which of these files should appear between Chappell-Murray, Inc. and Gigi Arts?
    A. C Q Service Inc., E&E Life Insurance, and Emcrisco
    B. Emcrisco, E&E Life Insurance, and Gordon, Jon & Associates
    C. E&E Life Insurance, and Emcrisco
    D. Emcrisco and Gordon, Jon & Associates

12.____

13. Which of these files should appear between Gordon, Jon & Associates and SOS Plumbing?
    A. Gigi Arts
    B. Schmidt, J.B. Co.
    C. Choices A and B
    D. None of the above

13.____

14. Each of the choices lists the four files in their proper alphabetical order EXCEPT
    A. E&E Life Insurance; Gigi Arts; Gordon, Jon & Associates; SOS Plumbing
    B. E&E Life Insurance; Emcrisco; Gigi Arts; SOS Plumbing
    C. Emcrisco; Gordon, Jon & Associates; SOS Plumbing; Schmidt, J.B. Co.
    D. Emcrisco; Gigi Arts; Gordon, Jon & Associates; SOS Plumbing

14.____

15. Which of the choices lists the four files in their proper alphabetical order?
    A. Gigi Arts; Gordon, Jon & Associates; SOS Plumbing; Schmidt, J.B. Co.
    B. Gordon, Jon & Associates; Gigi Arts; Schmidt, J.B. Co.; SOS Plumbing
    C. Gordon, Jon & Associates; Gigi Arts; SOS Plumbing; Schmidt, J.B. Co.
    D. Gigi Arts; Gordon, Jon & Associates; Schmidt, J.B. Co.; SOS Plumbing

15.____

16. The alphabetical filing order of two businesses with identical names is determined by the
    A. length of time each business has been operating
    B. addresses of the businesses
    C. last name of the company president
    D. no one of the above

16.____

17. In an alphabetical filing system, if a business name includes a number, it should be
    A. disregarded
    B. considered a number and placed at the end of an alphabetical section
    C. treated as though it were written in words and alphabetized accordingly
    D. considered a number and placed at the beginning of an alphabetical section

17.____

18. If a business name includes a contraction (such as *don't* or *it's*), how should that word be treated in an alphabetical system?
    A. Divide the word into its separate parts and treat it as two words
    B. Ignore the letters that come after the apostrophe
    C. Ignore the word that contains the contraction
    D. Ignore the apostrophe and consider all letters in the contraction

18.____

19. In what order should the parts of an address be considered when using an alphabetical filing system?   19._____
    A. City or town; state; street name; house or building number
    B. State; city or town; street name; house or building number
    C. House or building number; street name; city or town; state
    D. Street name; city or town; state

20. A business record should be cross-referenced when a(n)   20._____
    A. organization is known by an abbreviated name
    B. business has a name change because of a sale, incorporation, or other reason
    C. business is known by a *coined* or common name which differs from a dictionary spelling
    D. all of the above

21. A geographical filing system is MOST effective when   21._____
    A. location is more important than name
    B. many names or titles sound alike
    C. dealing with companies who have offices all over the world
    D. filing personal and business files

Questions 22-25.

DIRECTIONS: Questions 22 through 25 are to be answered on the basis of the list of items below, which are to be filed geographically. Organize the items geographically and then answer the questions.

       I. University Press at Berkeley, U.S.
     II. Maria Sanchez, Mexico City, Mexico
    III. Great Expectations Ltd. in London, England
    IV. Justice League, Cape Town, South Africa, Africa
     V. Crown Pearls Ltd. in London, England
    VI. Joseph Prasad in London, England

22. Which of the following arrangements of the items is composed according to the policy of: *Continent, Country, City, Firm or Individual Name*?   22._____
    A. V, III, IV, VI, II, I   B. IV, V, III, VI, II, I
    C. I, IV, V, III, VI, II   D. IV, V, III, VI, I, II

23. Which of the following files is arranged according to the policy of: *Continent, Country, City, Firm or Individual Name*?   23._____
    A. South Africa; Africa; Cape Town; Justice League
    B. Mexico; Mexico City; Maria Sanchez
    C. North America; United States; Berkeley; University Press
    D. England; Europe; London; Prasad, Joseph

24. Which of the following arrangements of the items is composed according to the policy of: *Country, City, Firm or Individual Name*?   24.____
    A. V, VI, III, II, IV, I
    B. I, V, VI, III, II, IV
    C. VI, V, III, II, IV, I
    D. V, III, VI, II, IV, I

25. Which of the following files is arranged according to a policy of: *Country, City, Firm or Individual Name*?   25.____
    A. England; London; Crown Pearls Ltd.
    B. North America; United States; Berkeley; University Press
    C. Africa; Cape Town; Justice League
    D. Mexico City; Mexico; Maria Sanchez

26. Under which of the following circumstances would a phonetic filing system be MOST effective?   26.____
    A. When the person in charge of filing can't spell very well
    B. With large files with names that sound alike
    C. With large files with names that are spelled alike
    D. All of the above

Questions 27-29.

DIRECTIONS: Questions 27 through 29 are to be answered on the basis of the following list of numerical files.

    I.   391-023-100
    II. 361-132-170
    III. 385-732-200
    IV. 381-432-150
    V.   391-632-387
    VI. 361-423-303
    VII. 391-123-271

27. Which of the following arrangements of the files follows a consecutive-digit system?   27.____
    A. II, III, IV, I   B. I, V, VII, III   C. II, IV, III, I   D. III, I, V, VII

28. Which of the following arrangements follows a terminal-digit system?   28.____
    A. I, VII, II, IV, III
    B. II, I, IV, V, VII
    C. VII, VI, V, IV, III
    D. I, IV, II, III, VII

29. Which of the following lists follows a middle-digit system?   29.____
    A. I, VII, II, VI, IV, V, III
    B. I, II, VII, IV, VI, V, III
    C. VII, II, I, III, V, VI, IV
    D. VII, I, II, IV, VI, V, III

Questions 30-31.

DIRECTIONS: Questions 30 and 31 are to be answered on the basis of the following information.

   I. Reconfirm Laura Bates appointment with James Caldecort on December 12 at 9:30 A.M.
   II. Laurence Kinder contact Julia Lucas on August 3 and set up a meeting for week of September 23 at 4 P.M.
   III. John Lutz contact Larry Waverly on August 3 and set up appointment for September 23 at 9:30 A.M.
   IV. Call for tickets for Gerry Stanton August 21 for New Jersey on September 23, flight 143 at 4:43 P.M.

30. A chronological file for the above information would be 30.____
    A. IV, III, II, I   B. III, II, IV, I   C. IV, II, III, I   D. III, I, II, IV

31. Using the above information, a chronological file for the date September 23 would be 31.____
    A. II, III, IV   B. III, I, IV   C. III, II, IV   D. IV, III, II

Questions 32-34.

DIRECTIONS: Questions 32 through 34 are to be answered on the basis of the following information.

   I. Call Roger Epstein, Ashoke Naipaul, Jon Anderson, and Sara Washingon on April 19 at 1:00 P.M. to set up meeting with Alika D'Ornay for June 6 in New York.
   II. Call Martin Ames before noon on April 19 to confirm afternoon meeting with Bob Greenwood on April 20th.
   III. Set up meeting room at noon for 2:30 P.M. meeting on April 19th.
   IV. Ashley Stanton contact Bob Greenwood at 9:00 A.M. on April 20 and set up meeting for June 6 at 8:30 A.M.
   V. Carol Guiland contact Shelby Van Ness during afternoon of April 20 and set up meeting for June 6 at 10:00 A.M.
   VI. Call airline and reserve tickets on June 6 for Roger Epstein trip to Denver on July 8.
   VII. Meeting at 2:30 P.M. on April 19th.

32. A chronological file for all of the above information would be 32.____
    A. II, I, III, VII, V, IV, VI   B. III, VII, II, I, IV, V, VI
    C. III, VII, I, II, V, IV, VI   D. II, III, I, VII, IV, V, VI

33. A chronological file for the date of April 19th would be 33.____
    A. II, III, VII, I   B. II, III, I, VII   C. VII, I, III, II   D. III, VII, I, II

34. Add the following information to the file, and then create a chronological file for April 20th: VIII. April 20: 3:00 P.M. meeting between Bob Greenwood and Martin Ames.
    A. IV, V, VIII   B. IV, VIII, V   C. VIII, V, IV   D. V, IV, VIII

35. The PRIMARY advantage of computer records over a manual system is
    A. speed of retrieval
    B. accuracy
    C. cost
    D. potential file loss

KEY (CORRECT ANSWERS)

1.	B	11.	D	21.	A	31.	C
2.	C	12.	C	22.	B	32.	D
3.	D	13.	B	23.	C	33.	B
4.	A	14.	C	24.	D	34.	A
5.	D	15.	D	25.	A	35.	A
6.	C	16.	B	26.	B		
7.	B	17.	C	27.	C		
8.	B	18.	D	28.	D		
9.	C	19.	A	29.	A		
10.	D	20.	D	30.	B		

PREPARING WRITTEN MATERIAL

PARAGRAPH REARRANGEMENT
COMMENTARY

The sentences that follow are in scrambled order. You are to rearrange them in proper order and indicate the letter choice containing the correct answer at the space at the right.

Each group of sentences in this section is actually a paragraph presented in scrambled order. Each sentence in the group has a place in that paragraph; no sentence is to be left out. You are to read each group of sentences and decide upon the best order in which to put the sentences so as to form a well-organized paragraph.

The questions in this section measure the ability to solve a problem when all the facts relevant to its solution are not given.

More specifically, certain positions of responsibility and authority require the employee to discover connection between events sometimes, apparently, unrelated. In order to do this, the employee will find it necessary to correctly infer that unspecified events have probably occurred or are likely to occur. This ability becomes especially important when action must be taken on incomplete information.

Accordingly, these questions require competitors to choose among several suggested alternatives, each of which presents a different sequential arrangement of the events. Competitors must choose the MOST logical of the suggested sequences.

In order to do so, they may be required to draw on general knowledge to infer missing concepts or events that are essential to sequencing the given events. Competitors should be careful to infer only what is essential to the sequence. The plausibility of the wrong alternatives will always require the inclusion of unlikely events or of additional chains of events which are NOT essential to sequencing the given events.

It's very important to remember that you are looking for the best of the four possible choices, and that the best choice of all may not even be one of the answers you're given to choose from.

There is no one right way to solve these problems. Many people have found it helpful to first write out the order of the sentences, as they would have arranged them, on their scrap paper before looking at the possible answers. If their optimum answer is there, this can save them some time. If it isn't, this method can still give insight into solving the problem. Others find it most helpful to just go through each of the possible choices, contrasting each as they go along. You should use whatever method feels comfortable and works for you.

While most of these types of questions are not that difficult, we've added a higher percentage of the difficult type, just to give you more practice. Usually there are only one or two questions on this section that contain such subtle distinctions that you're unable to answer confidently. And you then may find yourself stuck deciding between two possible choices, neither of which you're sure about.

EXAMINATION SECTION
TEST 1

DIRECTIONS: The following groups of sentences need to be arranged in an order that makes sense. Select the letter preceding the sequence that represents the BEST sentence order. *PRINT THE LETTER OF THE CORRECT ANSWER IN THE SPACE AT THE RIGHT.*

1.
   I. The keyboard was purposely designed to be a little awkward to slow typists down.
   II. The arrangement of letters on the keyboard of a typewriter was not designed for the convenience of the typist.
   III. Fortunately, no one is suggesting that a new keyboard be designed right away.
   IV. If one were, we would have to learn to type all over again.
   V. The reason was that the early machines were slower than the typists and would jam easily.
   The CORRECT answer is:
   A. I, III, IV, II, V
   B. II, V, I, IV, III
   C. V, I, II, III, IV
   D. II, I, V, III, IV

   1.____

2.
   I. The majority of the new service jobs are part-time or low-paying.
   II. According to the U.S. Bureau of Labor Statistics, jobs in the service sector constitute 72% of all jobs in this country.
   III. If more and more workers receive less and less money, who will buy the goods and services needed to keep the economy going?
   IV. The service sector is by far the fastest growing part of the United States economy.
   V. Some economists look upon this trend with great concern.
   The CORRECT answer is:
   A. II, IV, I, V, III
   B. II, III, IV, I, V
   C. V, IV, II, III, I
   D. III, I, II, IV, V

   2.____

3.
   I. They can also affect one's endurance.
   II. This can stabilize blood sugar levels, and ensure that the brain is receiving a steady, constant, supply of glucose, so that one is *hitting on all cylinders* while taking the test.
   III. By food, we mean real food, not junk food or unhealthy snacks.
   IV. For this reason, it is important not to skip a meal, and to bring food with you to the exam.
   V. One's blood sugar levels can affect how clearly one is able to think and concentrate during an exam.
   The CORRECT answer is:
   A. V, IV, II, III, I
   B. V, II, I, IV, III
   C. V, I, IV, III, II
   D. V, IV, I, III, II

   3.____

4. I. Those who are the embodiment of desire are absorbed in material quests, and those who are the embodiment of feeling are warriors who value power more than possession.
    II. These qualities are in everyone, but in different degrees.
    III. But those who value understanding yearn not for goods or victory, but for knowledge.
    IV. According to Plato, human behavior flows from three main sources: desire, emotion, and knowledge.
    V. In the perfect state, the industrial forces would produce but not rule, the military would protect but not rule, and the forces of knowledge, the philosopher kings, would reign.
    The CORRECT answer is:
    A. IV, V, I, II, III
    B. V, I, II, III, IV
    C. IV, III, II, I, V
    D. IV, II, I, III, V

5. I. Of the more than 26,000 tons of garbage produced daily in New York City, 12,000 tons arrive daily at Fresh Kills.
    II. In a month, enough garbage accumulates there to fill the Empire State Building.
    III. In 1937, the Supreme Court halted the practice of dumping the trash of New York City into the sea.
    IV. Although the garbage is compacted, in a few years the mounds of garbage at Fresh Kills will be the highest points south of Maine's Mount Desert Island on the Eastern Seaboard.
    V. Instead, tugboats now pull barges of much of the trash to Staten Island and the largest landfill in the world, Fresh Kills.
    The CORRECT answer is:
    A. III, V, IV, I, II
    B. III, V, II, IV, I
    C. III, V, I, II, IV
    D. III, II, V, IV, I

6. I. Communists rank equality very high, but freedom very low.
    II. Unlike communists, conservatives place a high value on freedom and a very low value on equality.
    III. A recent study demonstrated that one way to classify people's political beliefs is to look at the importance placed on two words: freedom and equality.
    IV. Thus, by demonstrating how members of these groups feel about the two words, the study has proved to be useful for political analysts in several European countries.
    V. According to the study, socialists and liberals rank both freedom and equality very high, while fascists rate both very low.
    The CORRECT answer is:
    A. III, V, I, II, IV
    B. V, IV, III, I, II
    C. III, V, IV, II, I
    D. III, I, II, IV, V

7. I. "Can there be anything more amazing than this?"
    II. If the riddle is successfully answered, his dead brothers will be brought back to life.
    III. "Even though man sees those around him dying every day," says Dharmaraj, "he still believes and acts as if he were immortal."
    IV. "What is the cause of ceaseless wonder?" asks the Lord of the Lake.
    V. In the ancient epic, The Mahabharata, a riddle is asked of one of the Pandava brothers.
    The CORRECT answer is:
    A. V, II, I, IV, III
    B. V, IV, III, I, II
    C. V, II, IV, III, I
    D. V, II, IV, I, III

8. I. On the contrary, the two main theories—the cooperative (neoclassical) theory and the radical (labor theory)—clearly rest on very different assumptions, which have very different ethical overtones.
    II. The distribution of income is the primary factor in determining the relative levels of material well-being that different groups or individuals attain.
    III. Of all issues in economics, the distribution of income is one of the most controversial.
    IV. The neoclassical theory tends to support the existing income distribution (or minor changes), while the labor theory ends to support substantial changes in the way income is distributed.
    V. The intensity of the controversy reflects the fact that different economic theories are not purely neutral, *detached* theories with no ethical or moral implications.
    The CORRECT answer is:
    A. II, I, V, IV, III
    B. III, II, V, I, IV
    C. III, V, II, I, IV
    D. III, V, IV, I, II

9. I. The pool acts as a broker and ensures that the cheapest power gets used first.
    II. Every six seconds, the pool's computer monitors all of the generating stations in the state and decides which to ask for more power and which to cut back.
    III. The buying and selling of electrical power is handled by the New York Power Pool in Guilderland, New York.
    IV. This is to the advantage of both the buying and selling utilities.
    V. The pool began operation in 1970, and consists of the state's eight electric utilities.
    The CORRECT answer is:
    A. V, I, II, III, IV
    B. IV, II, I, III, V
    C. III, V, I, IV, II
    D. V, III, IV, II, I

10. I. Modern English is much simpler grammatically than Old English.
    II. Finnish grammar is very complicated; there are some fifteen cases, for example.
    III. Chinese, a very old language, may seem to be the exception, but it is the great number of characters/words that must be mastered that makes it so difficult to learn, not its grammar.
    IV. The newest literary language—that is, written as well as spoken—is Finish, whose literary roots go back only to about the middle of the nineteenth century.
    V. Contrary to popular belief, the longer a language is been in use the simpler its grammar—not the reverse.
    The CORRECT answer is:
    A. IV, I, II, III, V
    B. V, I, IV, II, III
    C. I, II, IV, III, V
    D. IV, II, III, I, V

KEY (CORRECT ANSWERS)

1. D   6. A
2. A   7. C
3. C   8. B
4. D   9. C
5. C   10. B

TEST 2

DIRECTIONS: This type of question tests your ability to recognize accurate paraphrasing, well-constructed paragraphs, and appropriate style and tone. It is important that the answer you select contains only the facts or concepts given in the original sentences. It is also important that you be aware of incomplete sentences, inappropriate transitions, unsupported opinions, incorrect usage, and illogical sentence order. Paragraphs that do not include all the necessary facts and concepts, that distort them, or that add new ones are not considered correct.

The format for this section may vary. Sometimes, long paragraphs are given, and emphasis is placed on style and organization. Our first five questions are of this type. Other times, the paragraphs are shorter, and there is less emphasis on style and more emphasis on accurate representation of information. Our second group of five questions are of this nature.

For each of Questions 1 through 10, select the paragraph that BEST expresses the ideas contained in the sentences above it. *PRINT THE LETTER OF THE CORRECT ANSWER IN THE SPACE AT THE RIGHT.*

1.
   I. Listening skills are very important for managers.
   II. Listening skills are not usually emphasized.
   III. Whenever managers are depicted in books, manuals or the media, they are always talking, never listening.
   IV. We'd like you to read the enclosed handout on listening skills and to try to consciously apply them this week.
   V. We guarantee they will improve the quality of your interactions.

   A. Unfortunately, listening skills are not usually emphasized for managers. Managers are always depicted as talking, never listening. We'd like you to read the enclosed handout on listening skills. Please try to apply these principles this week. If you do, we guarantee they will improve the quality of your interactions.
   B. The enclosed handout on listening skills will be important improving the quality of your interactions. We guarantee it. All you have to do is take sometime this week to read and to consciously try to apply the principles. Listening skills are very important for manages, but they are not usually emphasized. Whenever managers are depicted in books, manuals or the media, they are always talking, never listening.
   C. Listening well is one of the most important skills a manager can have, yet it's not usually given much attention. Think about any representation of managers in books, manuals, or in the media that you may have seen. They're always talking, never listening. We'd like you to read the enclosed handout on listening skills and consciously try to apply them the rest of the week. We guarantee you will see a difference in the quality of your interactions.

1.____

143

D. Effective listening, one very important tool in the effective manager's arsenal, is usually not emphasized enough. The usual depiction of managers in books, manuals or the media is one in which they are always talking, never listening. We'd like you to read the enclosed handout and consciously try to apply the information contained therein throughout the rest of the week. We feel sure that you will see a marked difference in the quality of your interactions.

2. I. Chekhov wrote three dramatic masterpieces which share certain themes and formats: <u>Uncle Vanya</u>, <u>The Cherry Orchard</u>, and <u>The Three Sisters</u>.
    II. They are primarily concerned with the passage of time and how this erodes human aspirations.
    III. The plays are haunted by the ghosts of the wasted life.
    IV. The characters are concerned with life's lesser problems; however, such as the inability to make decisions, loyalty to the wrong cause, and the inability to be clear.
    V. This results in sweet, almost aching, type of a sadness referred to as Chekhovian.

2.____

   A. Chekhov wrote three dramatic masterpieces: <u>Uncle Vanya</u>, <u>The Cherry Orchard</u>, and <u>The Three Sisters</u>. These masterpieces share certain themes and formats: the passage of time, how time erodes human aspirations, and the ghosts of wasted life. Each masterpiece is characterized by a sweet, almost aching, type of sadness that has become known as Chekhovian. The sweetness of this sadness hinges on the fact that it is not the great tragedies of life which are destroying these characters, but their minor flaws: indecisiveness, misplaced loyalty, unclarity.
   B. <u>The Cherry Orchard</u>, <u>Uncle Vanya</u>, and <u>The Three Sisters</u> are three dramatic masterpieces written by Chekhov that use similar formats to explore a common theme. Each is primarily concerned with the way that passing time wears down human aspirations, and each is haunted by the ghosts of the wasted life. The characters are shown struggling futilely with the lesser problems of life: indecisiveness, loyalty to the wrong cause, and the inability to be clear. These struggles create a mood of sweet, almost aching, sadness that has become known as Chekhovian.
   C. Chekhov's dramatic masterpieces are, along with <u>The Cherry Orchard</u>, <u>Uncle Vanya</u>, and <u>The Three Sisters</u>. These plays share certain thematic and formal similarities. They are concerned most of all with the passage of time and the way in which time erodes human aspirations. Each play is haunted by the specter of the wasted life. Chekhov's characters are caught, however, by life's lesser snares: indecisiveness, loyalty to the wrong cause, and unclarity. The characteristic mood is a sweet, almost aching type of sadness that has come to be known as Chekhovian.
   D. A Chekhovian mood is characterized by sweet, almost aching, sadness. The term comes from three dramatic tragedies by Chekhov which revolve around the sadness of a wasted life. The three masterpieces (<u>Uncle Vanya</u>, <u>The Three Sisters</u>, and <u>The Cherry Orchard</u>) share the same

theme and format. The plays are concerned with how the passage of time erodes human aspirations. They are peopled with characters who are struggling with life's lesser problems. These are people who are indecisive, loyal to the wrong causes, or are unable to make themselves clear.

3. I. Movie previews have often helped producers decide which parts of movies they should take out or leave in.
    II. The first 1933 preview of <u>King Kong</u> was very helpful to the producers because many people ran screaming from the theater and would not return when four men first attacked by Kong were eaten by giant spiders.
    III. The 1950 premiere of <u>Sunset Boulevard</u> resulted in the filming of an entirely new beginning, and a delay of six months in the film's release.
    IV. In the original opening scene, William Holden was in a morgue talking with thirty-six other "corpses" about the ways some of them had died.
    V. When he began to tell them of his life with Gloria Swanson, the audience found this hilarious, instead of taking the scene seriously.

3. ____

   A. Movie previews have often helped producers decide what parts of movies they should leave in or take out. For example, the first preview of <u>King Kong</u> in 1933 was very helpful. In one scene, four men were first attacked by Kong and then eaten by giant spiders. Many members of the audience ran screaming from the theater and would not return. The premiere of the 1950 film <u>Sunset Boulevard</u> was also very helpful. In the original opening scene, William Holden was in a morgue with thirty-six other "corpses," discussing the ways some of them had died. When he began to tell them of his life with Gloria Swanson, the audience found this hilarious. They were supposed to take the scene seriously. The result was a delay of six months in the release of the film while a new beginning was added.
   B. Movie previews have often helped producers decide whether they should change various parts of a movie. After the 1933 preview of <u>King Kong</u>, a scene in which four men who had been attacked by Kong were eaten by giant spiders was taken out as many people ran screaming from the theater and would not return. The 1950 premiere of <u>Sunset Boulevard</u> also led to some changes. In the original opening scene, William Holden was in a morgue talking with thirty-six other "corpses" about the ways some of them had died. When he began to tell them of his life with Gloria Swanson, the audience found this hilarious, instead of taking the scene seriously.
   C. What do <u>Sunset Boulevard</u> and <u>King Kong</u> have in common? Both show the value of using movie previews to test audience reaction. The first 1933 preview of <u>King Kong</u> showed that a scene showing four men being eaten by giant spiders after having been attacked by Kong was too frightening for many people. They ran screaming from the theater and couldn't be coaxed back. The 1950 premiere of <u>Sunset Boulevard</u> was also a scream, but not the kind the producers intended. The movie opens

4 (#2)

with William Holden lying in a morgue discussing the ways they had died with thirty-six other "corpses." When he began to tell them of his life with Gloria Swanson, the audience couldn't take him seriously. Their laughter caused a six-month delay while the beginning was rewritten.

D. Producers very often use movie previews to decide if changes are needed. The premiere of Sunset Boulevard in 1950 led to a new beginning and a six-month delay in film release. At the beginning, William Holden and thirty-six other "corpses" discuss the ways some of them died. Rather than taking this seriously, the audience thought it was hilarious when he began to tell them of his life with Gloria Swanson. The first 1933 preview of King Kong was very helpful for its producers because one scene so terrified the audience that many of them ran screaming from the theater and would not return. In this particular scene, four men who had first been attacked by Kong were eaten by giant spiders.

4. I. It is common for supervisors to view employees as "things" to be manipulated. 4.____
    II. This approach does not motivate employees, nor does the carrot-and-stick approach because employees often recognize these behaviors and resent them.
    III. Supervisors can change these behaviors by using self-inquiry and persistence.
    IV. The best managers genuinely respect those they work with, are supportive and helpful, and are interested in working as a team with those they supervise.
    V. They disagree with the Golden Rule that says "he or she who has the gold makes the rules."

    A. Some managers act as if they think the Golden Rule means "he or she who has the gold makes the rules." They show disrespect to employees by seeing them as "things" to be manipulated. Obviously, this approach does not motivate employees any more than the carrot-and-stick approach motivates them. The employees are smart enough to spot these behaviors and resent them. On the other hand, the managers genuinely respect those they work with, are supportive and helpful, and are interested in working as a team. Self-inquiry and persistence can change even the former type of supervisor into the latter.
    B. Many supervisors all into the trap of viewing employees as "things" to be manipulated, or try to motivate them by using a carrot-and-stick approach. These methods do not motivate employees, who often recognize the behaviors and resent them. Supervisors can change these behaviors, however, by using self-inquiry and persistence. The best managers are supportive and helpful, and have genuine respect for those with whom they work. They are interested in working as a team with those they supervise. To them, the Golden Rule is not "he or she who has the gold makes the rules."
    C. Some supervisors see employees as "things" to be used or manipulated using a carrot-and-stick technique. These methods don't work. Employees often see through them and resent them. A supervisor who

wants to change may do so. The techniques of self-inquiry and persistence can be used to turn him or her into the type of supervisor who doesn't think the Golden Rule is "he or she who has the gold makes the rules." They may become like the best managers who treat those with whom they work with respect and give them help and support. These are the manager who know how to build a team.

D. Unfortunately, many supervisors act as if their employees are objects whose movements they can position at will. This mistaken belief has the same result as another popular motivational technique—the carrot-and-stick approach. Both attitudes can lead to the same result—resentment from those employees who recognize the behaviors for what they are. Supervisors who recognize these behaviors can change through the use of persistence and the use of self-inquiry. It's important to remember that the best managers respect their employees. They readily give necessary help and support and are interested in working as a team with those they supervise. To these managers, the Golden Rule is not "he or she who has the gold makes the rules."

5. I. The first half of the nineteenth century produced a group of pessimistic poets—Byron, De Musset, Heine, Pushkin, and Leopardi.
    II. It also produced a group of pessimistic composers—Schubert, Chopin, Schumann, and even the later Beethoven.
    III. Above all, in philosophy, there was the profoundly pessimistic philosopher, Schopenhauer.
    IV. The Revolution was dead, the Bourbons were restored, the feudal barons were reclaiming their land, and progress everywhere was being suppressed, as the great age was over.
    V. "I thank God," said Goethe, "that I am not young in so thoroughly finished a world."

    A. "I thank God," said Goethe, "that I am not young in so thoroughly finished a world." The Revolution was dead, the Bourbons were restored, the feudal barons were reclaiming their land, and progress everywhere was being suppressed. The first half of the nineteenth century produced a group of pessimistic poets: Byron, De Musset, Heine, Pushkin, and Leopardi. It also produced pessimistic composers: Schubert, Chopin, Schumann. Although Beethoven came later, he fits into this group, too. Finally and above all, it also produced a profoundly pessimistic philosopher, Schopenhauer. The great age was over.
    B. The first half of the nineteenth century produced a group of pessimistic poets: Byron, De Musset, Heine, Pushkin, and Leopardi. It produced a group of pessimistic composers: Schubert, Chopin, Schumann, and even the later Beethoven. Above all, it produced a profoundly pessimistic philosopher, Schopenhauer. For each of these men, the great age was over. The Revolution was dead, and the Bourbons were restored. The feudal barons were reclaiming their land, and progress everywhere was being suppressed.

5.____

C. The great age was over. The Revolution was dead—the Bourbons were restored, and the feudal barons were reclaiming their land. Progress everywhere was being suppressed. Out of this climate came a profound pessimism. Poets, like Byron, De Musset, Heine, Pushkin, and Leopardi; composers, like Schubert, Chopin, Schumann, and even the later Beethoven; and above all, a profoundly pessimistic philosopher, Schopenauer. This pessimism which arose in the first half of the nineteenth century is illustrated by these words of Goethe, "I thank God that I am not young in so thoroughly finished a world."

D. The first half of the nineteenth century produced a group of pessimistic poets, Byron, De Musset, Heine, Pushkin, and Leopardi—and a group of pessimistic composers, Schubert, Chopin, Schumann, and the later Beethoven. Above it all, it produced a profoundly pessimistic philosopher, Schopenhauer. The great age was over. The Revolution was dead, the Bourbons were restored, the feudal barons were reclaiming their land, and progress everywhere was being suppressed. "I thank God," said Goethe, "that I am not young in so thoroughly finished a world."

6. I. A new manager sometimes may feel insecure about his or her competence in the new position.
   II. The new manager may then exhibit defensive or arrogant behavior towards those one supervises, or the new manager may direct overly flattering behavior toward one's new supervisor.

   A. Sometimes, a new manager may feel insecure about his or her ability to perform well in this new position. The insecurity may lead him or her to treat others differently. He or she may display arrogant or defensive behavior towards those he or she supervises, or be overly flattering to his or her new supervisor.
   B. A new manager may sometimes feel insecure about his or her ability to perform well in the new position. He or she may then become arrogant, defensive, or overly flattering towards those he or she works with.
   C. There are times when a new manager may be insecure about how well he or she can perform in the new job. The new manager may also behave defensive or act in an arrogant way towards those he or she supervises, or overly flatter his or her boss.
   D. Sometimes a new manager may feel insecure about his or her ability to perform well in the new position. He or she may then display arrogant or defensive behavior towards those they supervise, or become overly flattering towards their supervisors.

6.____

7. I. It is possible to eliminate unwanted behavior by bringing it under stimulus control—tying the behavior to a cue, and then never, or rarely, giving the cue.
   II. One trainer successfully used this method to keep an energetic young porpoise from coming out of her tank whenever she felt like it, which was potentially dangerous.
   III. Her trainer taught her to do it for a reward, in response to a hand signal, and then rarely gave the signal.

7.____

A. Unwanted behavior can be eliminated by tying the behavior to a cue, and then never, or rarely, giving the cue. This is called stimulus control. One trainer was able to use this method to keep an energetic young porpoise from coming out of her tank by teaching her to come out for a reward in response to a hand signal, and then rarely giving the signal.
B. Stimulus control can be used to eliminate unwanted behavior. In this method, behavior is tied to a cue, and then the cue is rarely, if ever, given. One trainer was able to successfully use stimulus control to keep an energetic young porpoise from coming out of her tank whenever she felt like it—a potentially dangerous practice. She taught the porpoise to come out for a reward when she gave a hand signal, and then rarely gave the signal.
C. It is possible to eliminate behavior that is undesirable by bringing it under stimulus control by tying behavior to a signal, and then rarely giving the signal. One trainer successfully used this method to keep an energetic porpoise from coming out of her tank, a potentially dangerous situation. Her trainer taught the porpoise to do it for a reward, in response to a hand signal, and then would rarely give the signal.
D. By using stimulus control, it is possible to eliminate unwanted behavior by tying the behavior to a cue, and then rarely or never give the cue. One trainer was able to use this method to successfully stop a young porpoise from coming out of her tank whenever she felt like it. To curb this potentially dangerous practice, the porpoise was taught by the trainer to come out of the tank for a reward, in response to a hand signal, and then rarely given the signal.

8.
I. There is a great deal of concern over the safety of commercial trucks, caused by their greatly increased role in serious accidents since federal deregulation in 1981.
II. Recently, 60 percent of trucks in New York and Connecticut and 70 percent of trucks in Maryland randomly stopped by state troopers failed safety inspections.
III. Sixteen states in the United States require no training at all for truck drivers.

8.____

A. Since federal deregulation in 1981, there has been a great deal of concern over the safety of commercial trucks, and their greatly increased role in serious accidents. Recently, 60 percent of trucks in New York and Connecticut, and 70 percent of trucks in Maryland failed safety inspections. Sixteen states in the United States require no training at all for truck drivers.
B. There is a great deal of concern over the safety of commercial trucks since federal deregulation in 1981. Their role in serious accidents has greatly increased. Recently, 60 percent of trucks randomly stopped in Connecticut and New York and 70 percent in Maryland failed safety inspections conducted by state troopers. Sixteen states in the United States provide no training at all for truck drivers.
C. Commercial trucks have a greatly increased role in serious accidents since federal deregulation in 1981. This has led to a great deal of concern.

Recently, 70 percent of trucks in Maryland and 60 percent of trucks in New York and Connecticut failed inspection of those that were randomly stopped by state troopers. Sixteen states in the United States require no training for all truck drivers.

D. Since federal deregulation in 1981, the role that commercial trucks have played in serious accidents has greatly increased, and this has led to a great deal of concern. Recently, 60 percent of trucks in New York and Connecticut, and 70 percent of trucks in Maryland randomly stopped by state troopers failed safety inspections. Sixteen states in the U.S. don't require any training for truck drivers.

9.
I. No matter how much some people have, they still feel unsatisfied and want more, or want to keep what they have forever.
II. One recent television documentary showed several people flying from New York to Paris for a one-day shopping spree to buy platinum earrings, because they were bored.
III. In Brazil, some people were ordering coffins that cost a minimum of $45,000 and are equipping them with deluxe stereos, televisions, and other graveyard necessities.

A. Some people, despite having a great deal, still feel unsatisfied and want more, or think they can keep what they have forever. One recent documentary on television showed several people enroute from Paris to New York for a one day shopping spree to buy platinum earrings, because they were bored. Some people in Brazil are even ordering coffins equipped with such graveyard necessities as deluxe stereos and televisions. The price of the coffins start at $45,000.

B. No matter how much some people have, they may feel unsatisfied. This leads them to want more, or to want to keep what they have forever. Recently, a television documentary depicting several people flying from New York to Paris for a one day shopping spree to buy platinum earrings. They were bored. Some people in Brazil are ordering coffins that cost at least $45,000 and come equipped with deluxe televisions, stereos and other necessary graveyard items.

C. Some people will be dissatisfied no matter how much they have. They may want more, or they may want to keep what they have forever. One recent television documentary showed several people, motivated by boredom, jetting from New York to Paris for a one-day shopping spree to buy platinum earrings. In Brazil, some people are ordering coffins equipped with deluxe stereos, televisions and other graveyard necessities. The minimum price for these coffins—$45,000.

D. Some people are never satisfied. No matter how much they have they still want more, or think they can keep what they have forever. One television documentary recently showed several people flying from New York to Paris for the day to buy platinum earrings because they were bored. In Brazil, some people are ordering coffins that cost $45,000 and are equipped with deluxe stereos, televisions and other graveyard necessities.

10. I. A television signal or video signal has three parts.
    II. Its parts are the black-and-white portion, the color portion, and the synchronizing (sync) pulses, which keep the picture stable.
    III. Each video source, whether it's a camera or a video-cassette recorder contains its own generator of these synchronizing pulses to accompany the picture that it's sending in order to keep it steady and straight.
    IV. In order to produce a clean recording, a video-cassette recorder must "lock-up" to the sync pulses that are part of the video it is trying to record, and this effort may be very noticeable if the device does not have gunlock.

   A. There are three parts to a television or video signal: the black-and-white part, the color part, and the synchronizing (sync) pulses, which keep the picture stable. Whether it's a video-cassette recorder or a camera, each video source contains its own pulse that synchronizes and generates the picture it's sending in order to keep it straight and steady. A video-cassette recorder must "lock up" to the sync pulses that are part of the video it's trying to record. If the device doesn't have gunlock, this effort must be very noticeable.
   B. A video signal or television is comprised of three parts: the black-and-white portion, the color portion, and the sync (synchronizing) pulses, which keep the picture stable. Whether it's a camera or a video-cassette recorder, each video source contains its own generator of these synchronizing pulses. These accompany the picture that it's sending in order to keep it straight and steady. A video-cassette recorder must "lock up" to the sync pulses that are part of the video it is trying to record in order to produce a clean recording. This effort may be very noticeable if the device does not have gunlock.
   C. There are three parts to a television or video signal: the color portion, the black-and-white portion, and the sync (synchronizing pulses). These keep the picture stable. Each video source, whether it's a video-cassette recorder or a camera, generates these synchronizing pulses accompanying the picture it's sending in order to keep it straight and steady. If a clean recording is to be produced, a video-cassette recorder must store the sync pulses that are part of the video it is trying to record. This effort may not be noticeable if the device does not have gunlock.
   D. A television signal or video signal has three parts: the black-and-white portion, the color portion, and the synchronizing (sync) pulses. It's the sync pulses which keep the picture stable, which accompany it and keep it steady and straight. Whether it's a camera or a video-cassette recorder, each video source contains its own generator of these synchronizing pulses. To produce a clean recording, a video-cassette recorder must "lock up" to the sync pulses that are part of the video it is trying to record. If the device does not have gunlock, this effort may be very noticeable.

10._____

KEY (CORRECT ANSWERS)

1. C
2. B
3. A
4. B
5. D
6. A
7. B
8. D
9. C
10. D

PREPARING WRITTEN MATERIAL
EXAMINATION SECTION
TEST 1

DIRECTIONS: Each of the sentences in this test may be classified under one of the following four categories:
    A. Faulty because of incorrect grammar or word usage
    B. Faulty because of incorrect punctuation
    C. Faulty because of incorrect capitalization or incorrect spelling
    D. Correct

Examine each sentence carefully to determine under which of the above four options it is best classified. Then, in the space to the right, print the capital letter preceding the option which is the BEST of the four suggested above. (Note that each faulty sentence contains but one type of error. Consider a sentence to be correct if it contains none of the types of errors mentioned, even though there may be other correct ways of expressing the same thought.)

1. He sent the notice to the clerk who you hired yesterday.   1._____

2. It must be admitted, however that you were not informed of this change.   2._____

3. Only the employee who have served in this grade for at least two years are eligible for promotion.   3._____

4. The work was divided equally between she and Mary.   4._____

5. He thought that you were not available at that time.   5._____

6. When the messenger returns; please give him this package.   6._____

7. The new secretary prepared, typed, addressed, and delivered, the notices.   7._____

8. Walking into the room, his desk can be seen at the rear.   8._____

9. Although John has worked here longer than She, he produces a smaller amount of work.   9._____

10. She said she could of typed this report yesterday.   10._____

11. Neither one of these procedures are adequate for the efficient performance of this task.   11._____

12. The typewriter is the tool of the typist; the cash register, the tool of the cashier.   12._____

13. "The assignment must be completed as soon as possible" said the supervisor. 13._____

14. As you know, office handbooks are issued to all new Employees. 14._____

15. Writing a speech is sometimes easier than to deliver it before an audience. 15._____

16. Mr. Brown our accountant, will audit the accounts next week. 16._____

17. Give the assignment to whomever is able to do it most efficiently. 17._____

18. The supervisor expected either your or I to file these reports. 18._____

KEY (CORRECT ANSWERS)

1.	A	11.	A
2.	B	12.	C
3.	D	13.	B
4.	A	14.	C
5.	D	15.	A
6.	B	16.	B
7.	B	17.	A
8.	A	18.	A
9.	C		
10.	A		

TEST 2

DIRECTIONS: Each of the sentences in this test may be classified under one of the following four categories:
- A. Faulty because of incorrect grammar or word usage
- B. Faulty because of incorrect punctuation
- C. Faulty because of incorrect capitalization or incorrect spelling
- D. Correct

Examine each sentence carefully to determine under which of the above four options it is best classified. Then, in the space to the right, print the capital letter preceding the option which is the BEST of the four suggested above. (Note that each faulty sentence contains but one type of error. Consider a sentence to be correct if it contains none of the types of errors mentioned, even though there may be other correct ways of expressing the same thought.)

1. The fire apparently started in the storeroom, which is usually locked. 1.____
2. On approaching the victim, two bruises were noticed by this officer. 2.____
3. The officer, who was there examined the report with great care. 3.____
4. Each employee in the office had a seperate desk. 4.____
5. All employees including members of the clerical staff, were invited to the lecture. 5.____
6. The suggested Procedure is similar to the one now in use. 6.____
7. No one was more pleased with the new procedure than the chauffeur. 7.____
8. He tried to persaude her to change the procedure. 8.____
9. The total of the expenses charged to petty cash were high. 9.____
10. An understanding between him and I was finally reached. 10.____

KEY (CORRECT ANSWERS)

1.	D	6.	C
2.	A	7.	D
3.	B	8.	C
4.	C	9.	A
5.	B	10.	A

TEST 3

DIRECTIONS: Each of the sentences in this test may be classified under one of the following four categories:
- A. Faulty because of incorrect grammar or word usage
- B. Faulty because of incorrect punctuation
- C. Faulty because of incorrect capitalization or incorrect spelling
- D. Correct

Examine each sentence carefully to determine under which of the above four options it is best classified. Then, in the space to the right, print the capital letter preceding the option which is the BEST of the four suggested above. (Note that each faulty sentence contains but one type of error. Consider a sentence to be correct if it contains none of the types of errors mentioned, even though there may be other correct ways of expressing the same thought.)

1. They told both he and I that the prisoner had escaped.   1.____

2. Any superior officer, who, disregards the just complaint of his subordinates, is remiss in the performance of his duty.   2.____

3. Only those members of the national organization who resided in the Middle West attended the conference in Chicago.   3.____

4. We told him to give the national organization assignment to whoever was available.   4.____

5. Please do not disappoint and embarass us by not appearing in court.   5.____

6. Although the office's speech proved to be entertaining, the topic was not relevent to the main theme of the conference.   6.____

7. In February all new officers attended a training course in which they were learned in their principal duties and the fundamental operating procedure of the department.   7.____

8. I personally seen inmate Jones threaten inmates Smith and Green with bodily harm if they refused to participate in the plot.   8.____

9. To the layman, who on a chance visit to the prison observes everything functioning smoothly, the maintenance of prison discipline may seem to be a relatively easily realizable objective.   9.____

10. The prisoners in cell block fourty were forbidden to sit on the cell cots during the recreation hour.   10.____

KEY (CORRECT ANSWERS)

1.	A	6.	C
2.	B	7.	A
3.	C	8.	A
4.	D	9.	D
5.	C	10.	C

TEST 4

DIRECTIONS: Each of the sentences in this test may be classified under one of the following four categories:
- A. Faulty because of incorrect grammar or word usage
- B. Faulty because of incorrect punctuation
- C. Faulty because of incorrect capitalization or incorrect spelling
- D. Correct

Examine each sentence carefully to determine under which of the above four options it is best classified. Then, in the space to the right, print the capital letter preceding the option which is the BEST of the four suggested above. (Note that each faulty sentence contains but one type of error. Consider a sentence to be correct if it contains none of the types of errors mentioned, even though there may be other correct ways of expressing the same thought.)

1. I cannot encourage you any. 1._____
2. You always look well in those sort of clothes. 2._____
3. Shall we go to the park? 3._____
4. The man whome he introduced was Mr. Carey. 4._____
5. She saw the letter laying here this morning. 5._____
6. It should rain before the Afternoon is over. 6._____
7. They have already went home. 7._____
8. That Jackson will be elected is evident. 8._____
9. He does not hardly approve of us. 9._____
10. It was he, who won the prize. 10._____

KEY (CORRECT ANSWERS)

1. A   6. C
2. A   7. A
3. D   8. D
4. C   9. A
5. A   10. B

TEST 5

DIRECTIONS: Each of the sentences in this test may be classified under one of the following four categories:
  A. Faulty because of incorrect grammar or word usage
  B. Faulty because of incorrect punctuation
  C. Faulty because of incorrect capitalization or incorrect spelling
  D. Correct

Examine each sentence carefully to determine under which of the above four options it is best classified. Then, in the space to the right, print the capital letter preceding the option which is the BEST of the four suggested above. (Note that each faulty sentence contains but one type of error. Consider a sentence to be correct if it contains none of the types of errors mentioned, even though there may be other correct ways of expressing the same thought.)

1. Shall we go to the park. 1.____
2. They are, alike, in this particular way. 2.____
3. They gave the poor man sume food when he knocked on the door. 3.____
4. I regret the loss caused by the error. 4.____
5. The students' will have a new teacher. 5.____
6. They sweared to bring out all the facts. 6.____
7. He decided to open a branch store on 33rd street. 7.____
8. His speed is equal and more than that of a racehorse. 8.____
9. He felt very warm on that Summer day. 9.____
10. He was assisted by his friend, who lives in the next house. 10.____

KEY (CORRECT ANSWERS)

1.	B	6.	A
2.	B	7.	C
3.	C	8.	A
4.	D	9.	C
5.	B	10.	D

TEST 6

DIRECTIONS: Each of the sentences in this test may be classified under one of the following four categories:
A. Faulty because of incorrect grammar or word usage
B. Faulty because of incorrect punctuation
C. Faulty because of incorrect capitalization or incorrect spelling
D. Correct

Examine each sentence carefully to determine under which of the above four options it is best classified. Then, in the space to the right, print the capital letter preceding the option which is the BEST of the four suggested above. (Note that each faulty sentence contains but one type of error. Consider a sentence to be correct if it contains none of the types of errors mentioned, even though there may be other correct ways of expressing the same thought.)

1. The climate of New York is colder than California. 1.____
2. I shall wait for you on the corner. 2.____
3. Did we see the boy who, we think, is the leader. 3.____
4. Being a modest person, John seldom talks about his invention. 4.____
5. The gang is called the smith street bos. 5.____
6. He seen the man break into the store. 6.____
7. We expected to lay still there for quite a while. 7.____
8. He is considered to be the Leader of his organization. 8.____
9. Although I recieved an invitation, I won't go. 9.____
10. The letter must be here some place. 10.____

KEY (CORRECT ANSWERS)

1. A   6. A
2. D   7. A
3. B   8. C
4. D   9. C
5. C   10. A

TEST 7

DIRECTIONS: Each of the sentences in this test may be classified under one of the following four categories:
- A. Faulty because of incorrect grammar or word usage
- B. Faulty because of incorrect punctuation
- C. Faulty because of incorrect capitalization or incorrect spelling
- D. Correct

Examine each sentence carefully to determine under which of the above four options it is best classified. Then, in the space to the right, print the capital letter preceding the option which is the BEST of the four suggested above. (Note that each faulty sentence contains but one type of error. Consider a sentence to be correct if it contains none of the types of errors mentioned, even though there may be other correct ways of expressing the same thought.)

1. I though it to be he.
2. We expect to remain here for a long time.
3. The committee was agreed.
4. Two-thirds of the building are finished.
5. The water was froze.
6. Everyone of the salesmen must supply their own car.
7. Who is the author of Gone With the Wind?
8. He marched on and declaring that he would never surrender.
9. Who shall I say called?
10. Everyone has left but they.

KEY (CORRECT ANSWERS)

1.	A	6.	A
2.	D	7.	B
3.	D	8.	A
4.	A	9.	D
5.	A	10.	D

TEST 8

DIRECTIONS: Each of the sentences in this test may be classified under one of the following four categories:
- A. Faulty because of incorrect grammar or word usage
- B. Faulty because of incorrect punctuation
- C. Faulty because of incorrect capitalization or incorrect spelling
- D. Correct

Examine each sentence carefully to determine under which of the above four options it is best classified. Then, in the space to the right, print the capital letter preceding the option which is the BEST of the four suggested above. (Note that each faulty sentence contains but one type of error. Consider a sentence to be correct if it contains none of the types of errors mentioned, even though there may be other correct ways of expressing the same thought.)

1. Who did we give the order to?
2. Send your order in immediately.
3. I believe I paid the Bill.
4. I have not met but one person.
5. Why aren't Tom, and Fred, going to the dance?
6. What reason is there for him not going?
7. The seige of Malta was a tremendous event.
8. I was there yesterday I assure you
9. Your ukulele is better than mine.
10. No one was there only Mary.

KEY (CORRECT ANSWERS)

1. A
2. D
3. C
4. A
5. B
6. A
7. C
8. B
9. C
10. A

TEST 9

DIRECTIONS: In each of the following groups of sentences, one of the four sentences is faulty in grammar, punctuation, or capitalization. Select the INCORRECT sentence in each case.

1. A. If you had stood at home and done your homework, you would not have failed in arithmetic.
    B. Her affected manner annoyed every member of the audience.
    C. How will the new law affect our income taxes?
    D. The plants were not affected by the long, cold winter, but they succumbed to the drought of summer.

1.____

2. A. He is one of the most able men who have been in the Senate.
    B. It is he who is to blame for the lamentable mistake.
    C. Haven't you a helpful suggestion to make at this time?
    D. The money was robbed from the blind man's cup.

2.____

3. A. The amount of children in this school is steadily increasing.
    B. After taking an apple from the table, she went out to play.
    C. He borrowed a dollar from me.
    D. I had hoped my brother would arrive before me.

3.____

4. A. Whom do you think I hear from every week?
    B. Who do you think is the right man for the job?
    C. Who do you think I found in the room?
    D. He is the man whom we considered a good candidate for the presidency.

4.____

5. A. Quietly the puppy laid down before the fireplace.
    B. You have made your bed; now lie in it.
    C. I was badly sunburned because I had lain too long in the sun.
    D. I laid the doll on the bed and left the room.

5.____

KEY (CORRECT ANSWERS)

1. A
2. D
3. A
4. C
5. A

www.ingramcontent.com/pod-product-compliance
Lightning Source LLC
Chambersburg PA
CBHW082044300426
44117CB00015B/2609